Real Gardener's True Confessions

REAL GARDENERS' TRUE CONFESSIONS

Pat Stone

A Storey Publishing Book

STOREY

Storey Communications, Inc.
Schoolhouse Road
Pownal, Vermont 05261

The mission of Storey Communications
is to serve our customers by publishing practical information
that encourages personal independence in harmony with the environment.

Edited by Deborah Burns
Cover and text design by Cynthia N. McFarland
Cover photographs by Steve Dixon
Text production by Nat Stout

Illustrations on pages 6, 12, 14, 17, 18, 19, 27, 32, 34, 35, 37, 45, 57, 61, 62, 64, 79, 80, 92, 101, 112, 132, 134, 137, 140 by Marilynne Roach; on pages 4, 8, 20, 21, 26, 39, 54, 74, 95, 103, 114, 117, 120, 138, 145, 146, 154, 158, 160 by Brigita Fuhrmann; on pages 26, 27, 28, 40, 66, 70, 71, 75, 82, 84, 94, 107, 130, 131, 132, 143, 144, 147 by Alison Kolesar; on pages 22, 56, 73, 88, 89, 90, 91, 93, 95, 96, 97, 103, 104, 106, 121, 155 by Judy Eliason; on pages 29, 74, 108, 126, 148, 149 by Elayne Sears; on pages 23, 80 by David Sylvester; on page 105 by Barbara Carter; on page 119 by Ralph Scott.

Indexed by Northwind Editorial Services

Copyright © 1996 by Pat Stone

The information in this book is true and complete to the best of our knowledge. All recommendations are made without guarantee on the part of the author or Storey Communications, Inc. The author and publisher disclaim any liability in connection with the use of this information. For additional information please contact Storey Communications, Inc., Schoolhouse Road, Pownal, Vermont 05261.

Storey Publishing books are available for special premium and promotional uses and for customized editions. For further information, please call the Custom Publishing Department at 1-800-793-9396.

Printed in the United States by RR Donnelley

10 9 8 7 6 5 4 3 2 1

Library of Congress Cataloging-in-Publication Data

Stone, Pat, 1949–
    Real gardeners' true confessions / Pat Stone.
       p.   cm.
    "A Storey Publishing book."
    ISBN 0-88266-946-X (pbk. : alk. paper)
    1. Gardening.   I. Title.
SB453.S6857 1996
635—dc20   96-27625
                              CIP

TABLE OF CONTENTS

DEDICATION

To God, my family, and my plants — for all they put up with.

ACKNOWLEDGMENTS

It's S.A.P. (Standard Acknowledgment Procedure) for all authors to give everybody else the credit for the good parts of a book and take the blame for all the mistakes. Well, once you've read this one, you'll know just what a mistake-prone gardener I am, so you won't find it hard to believe (or think it false modesty) that I am, indeed, the correct person to blame for the writing mistakes in this book. (Thank you, thank you.)

As for credit,
I'd like to thank my friend Katrina Nicke (of the Walt Nicke Co.)
for talking me into doing this . . .
Gwen Steege, Deborah Burns, and the gang at Storey Communications
for being willing to polish and publish this . . .
my ten-year-old daughter's soccer team for putting up with another father-coach
while I worked on this
(of course, the fact that he did a better job than I ever did shouldn't figure into it) . . .
and all the other gardeners
who were willing to let me share some of the mistakes they've made,
so I wouldn't have to look like the *only* grower who ever lived up to the motto:

"Good judgment comes from experience; experience comes from bad judgment."

BEFORE WE BEGIN . . .

I don't know what got you growing. Maybe it was a childhood memory, having your own home, or wanting a haven from an otherwise hectic life. Maybe a piece of ground pulled you aside and whispered, "Veritable English horticultural estate!" Whatever the reason, you've boldly made the leap and decided to start a garden. To raise some plants for homegrown food or beauty. To get out and commune with our leafy brothers and sisters in your own backyard. To garner some of that sense of peace that's supposed to rub off on you when you start gardening.

Excellent! Grow for it!

But *how* to get started? Gardening is one of those things that can seem simultaneously simple and complex — so easy that kindergartners can sprout beans in cups and so overwhelmingly complicated that every gardener, no matter how expert, still has a lot to learn. (As our most horticulturally oriented president, Thomas Jefferson, once put it, "Though an old man, I am but a young gardener.")

Well, it's my job to make the basics of gardening as clear as possible — and your job to get out there and start learning from the real teacher: experience. Shall we begin?

INTRODUCTION

I've been gardening for the last twenty-odd years. I was Garden Editor of *The Mother Earth News* magazine for over a decade. And I currently edit and publish a garden magazine of my own, *GreenPrints, "The Weeder's Digest."*

So I must be a bona fide expert gardener, right?

Wrong!

Let me tell you just a few of the mistakes I've made:

- I once weeded my wife's entire flower bed — by pulling out all the flowers instead of the weeds.
- I used to stunt the indoor seedlings I started every year by forgetting to fertilize them. When I finally realized that error, I almost killed my next set of starts — by *over*fertilizing them.
- I transplanted a lovely young beech tree from my neighbor's woods, then forgot to water it. (It died.)
- I have planted seeds too deep, forgotten to start fall crops until *after* frost, pruned ornamentals too much (and not at all!), fried spring seedlings by leaving them in

a closed cold frame on a sunny day, wounded . . .

Get the picture? I have made a *lot* of gardening mistakes. Mind you, I am gradually getting better at all this (i.e., I'm making *new* mistakes instead of just repeating the old ones). And it's certainly true that mistakes are a very effective way to learn.

But seeing your plants shrivel up and die because of some error you made is *not* a whole lot of fun. Especially when the disaster is something you could have easily avoided if you'd only known about it ahead of time. ("You mean you're supposed to *support* cleomes? Why didn't anybody tell me that before they all fell over?!")

That's the point of *Real Gardeners' True Confessions*. This book will not tell you how to coddle the exotic perennials of an all-white, three-season, English flower border. It won't dissect soil mixes for greenhouse market gardening in northern Vermont.

No, this book is going to take the basic skills of gardening that every gardener should know and go through them simply and clearly (perhaps even humorously). It's going to cover the main steps of each skill and the **Classic Mistakes** many of us have made mastering them. Its goal: to make you feel a little less foolish and garden a good bit more successfully by helping you avoid all of the most common home gardening faux pas.

After all, I — and a host of other gardeners — have already discovered the *wrong* ways to do the backbone skills of gardening. I want to spare you some of the agony I've been through, to keep you from repeating some of the dumb mistakes I've made.

That way you can become a more advanced gardener — and make more advanced mistakes! No, no, I mean, "and garden successfully ever after." Actually, of course, you'll probably end up somewhere between those two extremes. Every gardener (no matter how expert) still experiences his or her share of self-induced horticultural failures. (I recently heard about an archaeologist who persuaded a 2,000-year-old lotus seed to sprout. Under her care, the plant died in six months.)

The aim of this book is simply to help you make as few mistakes as possible, to help you multiply your successes and limit your embarrassments.

Sound good to you? Then let's put on our jeans, grab a spade, and get started.

Weeds of Wisdom. *Throughout the book, you'll find sentences in green italics sprouting up here and there like little weeds. These short, "volunteer" messages reveal common goofs many other gardeners have made. Trust me, you'd be wise to try to avoid them.*

True Horticultural Confessions

Just so you won't think, after reading twenty chapters of Stonian slip-ups, that I'm the only gardener in the world who messes up, I asked a bunch of other growers I know, including several Storey staffers, if they would be willing to bare their horticultural souls and share a goof or two *they've* made.

You know what? People jumped at the chance! Everyone I called or wrote was eager to share mishaps they'd had. Growers from next door all the way to Alaska — including some of the most famous and respected gardeners in the country — readily told on themselves, sharing errors both reasonable and downright ridiculous!

I collected all fifty-seven of their "True Horticultural Confessions" and have sprinkled them throughout the book (in boxes that look like this one). I hope you'll enjoy reading them as much as I did hearing them. Some will likely serve as warnings for mess-ups to avoid; others I can't imagine happening to you in a thousand years! But, sensible or extreme, they all serve to remind us that, as contributor Inez Castor of Griffin City, California, put it, "The most important tool a gardener can have is a sense of humor. Keep it oiled, but not too sharp. You don't want to hurt yourself."

GARDEN DRIES UP Because Hose Wouldn't Reach!

Want to start things off by making a mistake that your garden will never recover from? To give your plants a handicap they will never overcome? To stunt your chances for success — permanently? Do you (gasp!) want to commit the Mother of All Gardening Mistakes?

Put the garden in the wrong spot.

A whole host of shortcomings can be considered here, and it's pretty hard to avoid them all. Several of them can be mitigated or worked around, but one factor above all has to take priority: sunlight.

Sun Is Number One

I stunted my tomatoes by planting them in the shade.

Most vegetables and flowers need **eight or more hours of direct sunlight a day.** Now a slew of people have tried to tell

Sun's path

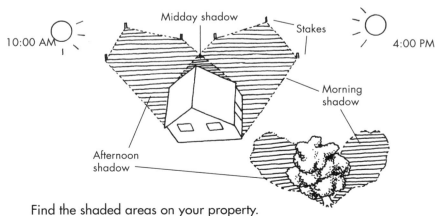

10:00 AM

Midday shadow

Stakes

4:00 PM

Morning shadow

Afternoon shadow

Find the shaded areas on your property.

themselves, "Oh, I know this spot along the side of the house is in shadow all day, but, heck, tomatoes'll grow all right here for ME." No, they won't. Sol plays no favorites (not even you). No sun, no crops. (There are, of course, many ornamental plants that love shady spots.)

How can you find a good sunny spot? Observe your property. Drive stakes to mark the shady areas as the sun moves across the sky in the morning, midday, and afternoon.

Take into account the time of year. If you do this near the summer solstice, June 21, the longest day of the year, the sun will be at its peak in the sky, so shadows will be the shortest they get all year. If you do it near the winter solstice, December 22, the shortest day of the year, the sun will be traveling in its lowest arc, and shadows will be the longest they ever get.

Choose your garden site only from areas that get enough sun. Mind you, shade during part of the day is fine. Indeed, in really hot areas of the country or during really hot times of the year, plants may appreciate a little shade. And some plants need less sun than others. As a general rule, vegetables that form fruits need a good eight to ten hours of direct sunlight a day, root crops need six to eight hours, and leaf crops may even get by on less. It's harder to generalize about flowers, but I'd venture (gulp!) that the bigger and flashier the flower, the more sun it needs to get that way.

All in all, sun makes plants run — and you can't ignore that fact.

There are other basic factors, and the more you can incorporate them into your choice of site, the less work you'll have to do to build a successful garden. But none is as critical as light.

Shady Doings

"If you love plants, you want to try to grow everything. But you can't grow plants in spots where they don't like to grow. You know that, I know that, but I don't always do it. When my husband and I moved into our new home five years ago, I planted a sun-loving tree peony in the darkest hole in our garden. It tried hard for a couple of years, but, sigh, by the third year, there weren't even any roots left."

— *Marty Ross of Kansas City, Missouri, a syndicated garden columnist for Universal Press as well as a regular garden columnist for the Kansas City Star*

The Closer to the House, the Better the Garden

I neglected my garden because it was too far away!

The old Chinese gardening proverb states: "The best fertilizer is the gardener's footsteps" — meaning, of course, that the key to success in a garden is giving it attention and energy. And the corollary to this proverb is: "The more footsteps it takes a gardener to get to the garden, the fewer footsteps he or she will be making *in* it."

And that's the truth: **the farther away the garden is, the less you'll end up doing in it.** If you can see your plot right out your window, or if you have to pass by it to get from your car to your house, you're easily and happily going to spend little moments in it here and there that will make a big difference in the end result, partly

The farther away the garden, the less successful it will be.

healthy plants. (Plants *are* what they eat, you know.) If you've got a wonderfully friable, fertile spot to choose from, great. Poor soil can be improved, of course, but it takes labor (work) and expense (money). So the better ground you start off with, the less improving you'll have to do.

Right away, you can see how this might conflict with the "the closer, the better" rule just above. Many a home is built on a foundation where all the topsoil was scraped away during construction and only hard subsoil left behind. Start your kitchen garden right outside the door in that kind of site and you might be sowing in slate.

How about this creative compromise? Put your main garden out where the better soil is, and build a raised bed for fresh herbs, cut flowers, or salad veggies right by the door. It's not too hard to create one fertile bed of soil (we'll get to it). That will give you some of the benefits of a close garden without having to restore an entire moonscape.

Drain the Rain

I drowned my plants by putting them in a soggy spot!

Avoid growing where your plants' roots will wallow in wetness. As Richard E. Bir, an expert horticulturist I know, once put it, "When I'm asked to diagnose an ailing plant, the most frequent culprit is soil drainage."

Roots need oxygen; indeed, one quarter of healthy soil is actually *air.* Soggy soil simply drowns roots.

Is the spot you're looking at too wet? You can tell by digging. If the soil looks dark red or brown, it probably drains well. Mottled soil or soil that's gray with yellow or red mixed in is a bad sign.

because half the time those "little moments" turn themselves into "little hours." (As one gardener I know, Eric Grissell, put it, "There's never enough time to do massive gardening tasks, but always enough to work endlessly at the small ones!")

Select Succulent Soil

I starved my plants by giving them poor soil!

Obviously, you'd prefer to garden in dark, rich, loose, loamy soil. Healthy soil makes for

Checking your site's drainage

For a more accurate drainage reading, take both ends off a 46-ounce can (a large juice can). Dig a 4-inch hole in the garden site, set the can in the hole, and pack dirt around the base of the can so water won't leak out. Now fill the can to the top with water, go away, and come back in one hour.

Did the water level in the can drop somewhere between 2 and 5 inches? Good — you have good drainage. Did it drop more than 5 inches? You have *excessive* drainage. (You'll either have to remedy that garden site with lots of organic matter or plan on doing a lot of irrigating.) Did the water level in the can hardly drop at all? You definitely have *poor* drainage.

Solution number one to a "poor-D" problem: **put your garden somewhere else.** (Make a nice ornamental bog garden at the first site, instead.) Trust me, this *is* the best solution.

If you must use this spot (you're stuck with the muck), you have two choices: **raised beds** or **French drains.** You can essentially garden on top of the bog by building walled, raised garden beds over it. This isn't really too bad an idea, because raised beds (as we'll discuss later) have a lot going for them.

Tackling the problem head on with a French drain (don't ask me why the French get credit for it) will take more work, but at least it's a one-time project. Dig a water-diverting trench 1 to 2 feet deep and 3 to 18 inches wide upslope from your garden site. It needs to drop ½ inch every 10 feet and have an outlet where the run-off won't do any harm (i.e., *not* your neighbor's backyard).

Digging is serious work; you may well want to rent a trenching machine from a tool rental shop. Make sure the trench goes at least 6 to 12 inches below the topsoil, into the hard

Calling King Edward! Your Geraniums are in!

"A lot of gardening mistakes have to do with plain old naiveté. When I first came to work at Logee's Greenhouses, I was taking care of the geraniums. I didn't know anything about geraniums. I thought all those names on the plants meant that they were reserved. When I saw some trays labeled 'Mrs. Henry Cox,' I wouldn't let anyone else touch them. I was going to hold them until she arrived to pick them up! Same with the flats of 'Mrs. Layal'.

"I began to wonder, though, when I came to 'Prince Rupert's' geraniums, and especially when I came across a tray labeled 'King Edward'. After all, he'd only been dead for 200 years!

"Another example of my horticultural, um, unsophistication came with a vegetable garden I once grew. My brother-in-law looked at the weeds coming up in my corn and uttered a Yankee phrase I'd never heard before: 'You better get that corn weeded before it goes back into the ground.'

"Well, you know, I thought that might be fun to watch. So I didn't weed the corn at all. The next time my brother-in-law dropped by, he snapped, 'Did I not tell you to weed that corn?'

"'I can't,' I replied. 'I'm waiting for it to go back in the ground!'"
— *Tovah Martin of Danielson, Connecticut, a gardening consultant at Logee's Greenhouses and Garden Editor for* Victoria *magazine*

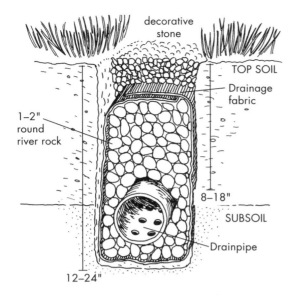

A French drain (in cross-section here) can divert excess water away from a site with poor drainage.

decorative stone

TOP SOIL

Drainage fabric

1–2" round river rock

8–18"

SUBSOIL

Drainpipe

12–24"

fabric around all this. You can then fill the rest of the trench with smaller, decorative stone (if you want the trench to drain surface water as well as groundwater) or dirt.

I hope you don't have to go to all this trouble. But if you must, well, once done and you're done with it.

By the way, a soggy soil problem is different from a surface runoff problem. You can solve the latter drainage problem fairly simply by hand digging a drainage ditch upslope from the garden. It shouldn't have to be very deep; ideally, you'll make it shallow and wide (a swale). That way, the rainwater diverter will be less likely to cave in *and* be less of a nuisance in your landscape.

subsoil. Line the entire trench with a long piece of drainage fabric (a product that blocks silt but lets water pass out). Then lay down a 3- to 6-inch layer of river rock. Put the drain (either corrugated black drainpipe or rigid, holed PVC) on top of the stone, making sure you still have that ½-inch per 10-foot drop. Cap the top end of the pipe and screen the bottom end (to keep out animals). Add more stone so the pipe is thoroughly covered, then wrap the drainage

Don't Forget the Weather

I exposed my garden to the elements!

Is your prevailing wind from the west? If so, your garden may do much better if there's a windbreak on that side of your plot. Harsh wind dries and chills plants. A good windbreak isn't completely solid, but lets some air through — and it will shield a distance downwind of twice its height.

Do you live at the edge of a valley? Frost — which, after all, is water — runs down-

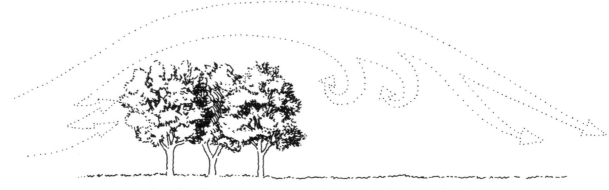

A windbreak will protect a distance downwind of twice its height.

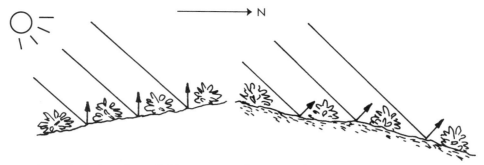

A south-facing slope (left) gets more direct sun than a north-facing slope (right).

hill. It likes to form (you might say "pool") at the bottom of a valley. So, surprisingly, people slightly upslope get more time between killing frosts than the folks in the flatland below. The moral here, then, is that if there's a hill on your property, you may well be better off growing on its side rather than at its bottom.

I made my life harder because I didn't make my garden easy to get to.

Speaking of slope, if your garden site tilts southward, it will get warmer sooner in spring than if it's flat (because it more directly faces the rays of the sun). Hillsiders in the North can thereby add weeks to their growing season if they plant on a southern slope.

By the same thinking, hilly Southerners can help *cool* their garden spots if they plant on the *north* side of slopes.

Can You Get There From Here?

Can you get things to the garden conveniently? Water — gotta have it. Put that garden down at the far corner of your property and you may need a mighty long hose. Compost, mulch, fertilizer — if you're driving these things home, wouldn't it be nice if you could then drive them right to the garden? You're probably smart enough to build your compost pile next to the garden so you can easily move that black gold from its spot to your plot, but is your forefocal (the lens of foresight) so sharp that you also put your compost pile where you can easily drive to it? Then when you come home with all those bags of curbside leaves or that truck full of manure, you can just back up to the bin and unload.

Where, too, will you put a toolshed? (Answer: as close to the garden as possible.)

Ground Not Covered

"We have a steep slope at home, which I envisioned filled in with ground cover. Unfortunately the plants never filled in and made it harder than ever to mow. It looked like a bunch of straggly plants stuck on this hill. The moral to me was, plan your garden carefully before you plant. I finally hired a neighborhood kid to dig one big hole in the middle of the hill and I moved all my plants there. My garden looks much more organized now."

— Allison Cranmer, Creative Coordinator at Storey Publishing

■ ■ ■ ■ ■

Well, class is over for now. Grab a spot with lots of sun, as close to the house as possible, with good soil and drainage, that takes into account your property's weather, and has good access for supplies — that's about it for Garden Siting 101. If it sounds simple, that's because it is. But simple doesn't mean trivial. Critical is more like it. Actually — and you can quote me — if there's a more ruinous mistake than making your garden in the wrong spot, I don't know what it is.

Perennial Problems

"I remember, at the first home I owned, how I wanted to have that beautiful perennial garden. But you can't always be sure a plant *is* a perennial if you just go by its common name. Plus, some plants that are perennials farther south grow only as annuals up here in Michigan's zone 5 climate. I grew plants like alyssum, carnation, and blue salvia that first year in my garden, and none of them came back the second year. I was crushed. I thought I'd never have a garden again.

"Now that I have a garden design business as well as my own garden at home, I get to see — and make — lots of mistakes. The old garden rule that you should never plant too big an area? I've broken that — I remember once sitting in a garden bed and crying because I wasn't able to keep up with it. I still break that rule — and have to try to talk my customers out of breaking it, as well. Really, 200 square feet is plenty for a new garden.

"I've seen so many people have problems with invasive plants that I now firmly believe every flower gardener should have a holding garden for trying new plants out. It could be in the vegetable garden, where you don't mind having to dig things up. In a perennial garden, it can take years to get out what you put in on one June day. I'm still struggling with showy primrose and gooseneck loosestrife in my garden — charming and nasty plants. And it's very hard to dig invasive plants out of a perennial bed without harming the plants you do want. I'm at risk of ruining a prized dogwood of mine trying to get the other plants around it out.

"Another mistake I — and many perennial gardeners — have made is to dig too close to pavement. I like deep, double-dug perennial flower beds. But if you dig like that close to pavement — a drive, a sidewalk, a patio path — in a few years, the soil under the pavement will start to collapse. Now I know to leave a good 8 inches of that compacted soil next to any area I don't want to see beginning to sink."

— *Janet Macunovich, author of* Caring for Perennials *and* Easy Garden Design *and the head of Perennial Favorites, a garden design business*

2. STARTING OFF ON THE WRONG FOOT

THE 7 DEADLY PITFALLS of Gardening

Gardener, stay that spade! Just because you've finished choosing the best of all possible sites for your garden doesn't mean you should rush right out and start digging up ground. A slew of preliminary decisions still need to be made. Yeah, there remains a veritable host of opportunities to start your garden off on the wrong foot.

Let's take a few moments to review some of the most basic faux pas. Experience may be the best teacher, but no one ever said it has to be *your* experience. You're welcome to take advantage of the many other gardeners — like me — who were kind enough to make these errors for you.

Pitfall #1: Starting Too Big

My tiller was too big for my hoe. I planted much more than I could possibly tend.

Starting too big is — what else? — the *big* beginning mistake. Just about the only people who avoid it are the ones who simply don't have the room to commit it. It's caused by combining beginner's overenthusiasm with that annual rampant infection, spring gardening fever.

This double fervor makes no area seem big enough for all you want to grow. We've all been guilty of having "eyes bigger than our stomachs," heaping too much food on our plates because we think we can eat it all. This is the horticultural equivalent: creating an overly large garden because you think, in the dead of winter or initial (actually, modest) flush of spring growth, you'll be able to manage it all.

However, that fails to take into account the little-discussed difference between plants' and people's energy curves. We people types get all excited and work like whirling dervishes in those sap-stirring weeks of early spring. Then summer comes along, and all that heat (and life's many other distractions) begins to lessen the time and effort we put into gardening. Many people's natural garden-energy curve is like a ski jump: starting off high and then heading downhill as the season advances.

Plants, though, are just the opposite. At first, seeds just sit under the soil — for days,

11

Pitfall #1: Starting too big

weeks, hardly *thinking* about growing. Finally they poke out a scrawny stem, a leaf or two, a week later another. As the weeks go by and the weather warms, the pace picks up a bit, but not much.

For a while there, early and midspring, you're way ahead of the game. It's a cinch to weed, to water, to mulch. Almost too easy. Why doesn't *everybody* garden? you wonder.

But the plants have just begun to grow. Plant energy, you see, is a slow-starting drag racer, a long-simmering volcano, the Photosynthesis Special starting down Track 97. Just when *your* energy is flagging with those dog days of summer, your garden is laying root rubber, blowing its sun-heated top, leaping off its horticultural tracks. There are flocks of flowers to deadhead, bushels of beans to harvest, waves of weeds to subdue.

The result? You suddenly have so much to do you can't keep up with it all. Gardening shifts from being an enjoyable outdoor activity to an overload of work. Either you burn yourself out doing all the equally pressing tasks or fall irrevocably behind and watch your garden become a horticultural junkyard of abandoned, overgrown vegetation.

Being overwhelmed by your garden is a widespread and truly disheartening experience. Many, many a gardener, old and new, has fallen into this trap. Just about the only way to avoid it is to **create the smallest garden you can let yourself make.** Remember, you can always make it bigger next year.

This is particularly true if you have grand landscaping plans for your whole yard. You say you want a vegetable garden here, a hedge of shrubs along the drive, a herb patch by the back door, a flower border along the fence, a miniature fruit farm out back? Do one *and only one* of those projects this year. Rome wasn't built in a day? Good gardens aren't grown in one year.

Pitfall #2:
Reinventing the Wheel

I fenced myself off as well as my garden.

Some of us, well, maybe we're a little shy, or a little too independent minded, or too book oriented, or too overconfident. Whatever the cause, we think we can do a bit of background reading and then figure out how to garden all on our own.

Bad idea. The fact is, no good gardener is an island. Why? Other area gardeners are your absolute best source of know-how (yes, even better than — ahem — me), not just because they may be more experienced than you, but because they *understand local growing conditions.* They know when it's really *safe* to assume your last spring frost has hit. They know which pests you'll have the worst troubles with. They know that, in your area, it's just not worth trying to grow peaches or plumeria. They know which plants will do well in shade, which can't tolerate that horrible drought, cold snap, flood, or heat wave that your area specializes in. They know what to grow in Your Town, USA — and how to grow it.

How do you find such sages? Look and ask. Do your neighbors garden? How about folks at church or the parents of your children's friends? Is there a beautiful yard a few streets over? Think of a horticultural question you'd like to ask its owners. Walk your (leashed) dog in that direction sometime when they're outside, and as you saunter by, follow a compliment with a query. Of course, there are local garden clubs to join and learn from, county agricultural extension people to ask, and local newspaper garden columnists or radio gardeners who desperately *need* people like you to ask them questions.

Fact is, as a whole, gardeners are the friend-liest, most helpful people you'll ever want to meet. Say a nice word about a plant, and they're likely to give you a cutting of it. Indeed, with just a little bit of outreach on your part, you'll soon discover that one of the best things you'll grow as a gardener is friendships.

The Goof That Made Good

"Probably the biggest mistake beginning gardeners make is to forget that small is beautiful, to try to grow too big a garden — or to miscalculate and buy too much seed for the garden they have.

"I did it when I was growing my first commercial garden on an acre of land. I bought *ten pounds* of pea seed to sow in 16 double rows. When I finished planting those rows, I still had five pounds of seed left. I didn't know what to do with it. Well, I had a 30x30-foot weedy area I wasn't using, so I just rototilled that under and broadcast the pea seeds all over it. They came up so quick and thickly, they smothered all the weeds. I didn't have to weed or water the area, yet it gave me more peas — and with less effort — than the rows I'd grown on purpose.

"That's when the idea of planting in wide rows came to me, an idea that's served me quite well over the years. So you might say this is one mistake that turned out for the good."

— Dick Raymond of Ferrisburg, Vermont, is one of our country's most famous gardeners. His classic The Joy of Gardening *has sold over a million copies, and he has been on numerous TV garden shows.*

Starting too early

Pitfall #3: Starting Too Early

I've sowed in March what I shouldn't have planted until May. I've set out tomatoes in April that shouldn't have seen the sun until June. I've let my impatience seduce me into buying impatiens when I had to shovel snow off my drive to get to the store.

If there were a horticultural confessional, you'd have to draw a number each spring before you could get in. Starting too early, like starting too big, is a direct effect of that ol' early-season garden fever. That first balmy spell of Indian spring hits, and — whammo! — we're popping pepper plants in the ground or setting out trays of tender ornamentals. Sure, our official frost-free date is close to a month away. But feel that sun! Smell that air! Let's go, sisters, it's planting time!

Well, all I can say is when those seeds rot in the ground, when the transplants grow in reverse, when that surprise (to you) frost levels all those tender crops and flowers — don't say Uncle Pat didn't warn you. (Tsk, tsk, tsk.)

If you can't resist gambling with nature, though, let me give you one tip: **do it with cool-season crops, not warm ones.** Broccoli, lettuce, peas, calendulas, four o'clocks — a bit of cold weather may slow them down, but usually it's not too likely to stop them. Heat-loving plants like tomatoes, corn, melons, cosmos, and zinnias are obviously more likely to succumb to nippy weather. And, surprisingly, if they do survive, they often won't do any better than the same plants started later, once the soil warms. Plants just don't grow well when the temperature's not to their suiting. They're fussy that way.

Do yourself a favor and humor them.

Pitfall #4:
Planting Only Once

I lived — and planted — only for today!

Other phrases I might have used to identify this mistake are "Plan in space, but not in time" or "Forget about fall." What they all mean is don't forget that there are *three* seasons to the garden year, not just one. This is especially true for vegetable gardens. The old idea that you plant the garden on Memorial Day and give it up on Labor Day has the advantage of simplicity and the disadvantage of giving you too much harvest at the end of the summer and none at all the rest of the year. (Sometimes it's hard to say which is worse.)

To avoid an all-or-nothing food garden, plan for a *succession* of plantings throughout the year. To avoid a bloom-all-at-once flower garden, choose flowers that bear at different times of the year. There are two aspects to this. The first is: **sow the same crop repeatedly**. Plant a short row of bush beans or lettuce every two weeks instead of a big planting all at once. Or achieve the same effect by simultaneously planting varieties that have different maturing dates — sow three blocks of early, midseason, and late sweet corn, for instance. This requires a little extra planning, but it's well worth it.

The second type of succession is: **start new crops throughout the growing season.** You don't need two or three gardens to do this; often you can use the same space that grew a spring crop for a summer or fall one, as well. Summer tomatoes can go in when spring spinach comes out, for instance.

I'll be honest — the hardest time for me to remember my own advice in this regard is during midsummer. In the sweltering days of July, I forget there *is* such a thing as cold weather — and if I want to enjoy some frost-sweetened lettuce, broccoli, kale, spinach, peas, and carrots, I'd better start growing them *now*. And I'll have to work extra hard in this hot weather to keep their seeds *constantly* moist until they germinate.

But, hey, just because *I* have trouble remembering to do this doesn't mean you have to.

Gardening on New York Time

"My husband was from New York; he went to New York State Agricultural College. When we moved out here to Oklahoma, we wanted to start a big garden. In fact, we bought the lot adjacent to us so we could really grow on a big scale.

"The only trouble was my husband didn't start planting until June. Everyone around these parts starts planting out in January or February. You see, though, he was still gardening on New York time, not Oklahoma time."

— Louise Riotte of Ardmore, Oklahoma, author of several books about gardening, including her famed book on companion planting, Carrots Love Tomatoes

Pitfall #5: Keeping Track of It All in Your Head

I trusted my memory, instead of my notebook.

Some of us are organized types. Tax receipts for 1967? They're in the third drawer on the left. Programming instructions for the VCR? Oh, they're in the box it came in, of course, and that box is . . . .

Those people will naturally keep good garden records, writing down when and where and variety and harvests and crop rotations and new pest solutions tried and new design ideas imagined and . . . *and* they will make fewer garden mistakes than the rest of us. So even if you don't balance your checkbook and are sure your kid's birth certificate is *somewhere,* you'll find it a really good idea to have a garden notebook and to write in it. Your entries don't have to rival government regulations for length — just a few pertinent notes with dates attached will help a great deal. Keep your notebook where you stash your hoe and trowel so you can write something while it's fresh in your mind. You know that old history saw: Those who don't remember the past are doomed to repeat it. Well, the gardeners who do remember their past growing mistakes and don't repeat them are the ones who wrote them down.

Mashed Potatoes — uh, Tomatoes

"Early in our gardening career, my husband was too early himself. He put out some young tomato plants, only to hear soon afterward that a frost was due. To protect the plants, he went out and carefully put a cardboard box on top of each plant. Then he put a rock on each box to hold it in place.

"That night the frost hit. It dampened all those top-heavy, or should I say rock-heavy, boxes so much that they all collapsed . . . and mashed every plant!"
— *Marty Figley, a gardening columnist in Birmingham, Michigan*

Pitfall #6: Neglecting to Fence

My garden could have had a sign on it: FREE PICKINGS FOR PESTS!

Let's say you spread ten-dollar bills all over your front yard and left them alone for twenty-three hours a day. How long do you think it would be before they all found homes in other people's pockets?

It's not safe to leave other kinds of green lying around, either. Why do we grow our own food and flowers? Because they're so much more tender and lush and tasty than most plants growing wild. Well, most wild animals can appreciate that taste difference even more than you can. Rabbits, raccoons, gophers, woodchucks, deer, cows (at least in my garden), possums, moles — whether you live in New York or Nevada, some varmints will be only too happy to enjoy the fruits of your labors.

I don't like fences, but it's awfully hard to raise a garden without one. The very word "garden" means "walled enclosure," and generally that's what it takes to have one. So if you want to try to raise plants without providing them with some sort of barrier for protection, be my guest. Then, speaking of guests, I hope your garden doesn't receive uninvited ones.

Pitfall #7: Letting Gardening Become Work

I became a slave to my salvias!

Let's define work as something you don't enjoy doing — or maybe something that, *after a certain point,* you don't enjoy doing. For instance, I don't mind doing some weeding. It gets you close to your plants, has an enjoyably ruthless quality all its own, and gives instantly visible results. But, hey, it does get tedious after a while.

Pitfall #6: Neglecting to fence

One trick to successful gardening is to look for ways to reduce the aspects of it that you least enjoy. I'd rather spend a few hours mulching my crops and flowers than weeding them all summer. I'd rather grow a small garden I can keep up with than a big one that gets to be too much to handle. I'd rather raise flowers that do well naturally in my climate than ones that need constant watering, staking, or pest policing to survive. I'd rather put a groundcover once in an area of the yard I don't use than mow it every week just to keep it under control.

So keep your eyes and mind open. Whenever a gardening task starts to get you down, think if there are other, easier ways to get the job done. See if other gardeners have different ways of handling the same situation. You'll never eliminate every chore (I don't think I'd want to, really), but it's a mistake not to keep looking for ways to boost the pleasures and minimize the bothers of gardening.

■ ■ ■ ■ ■

There you have it, Stone's Seven Starting-Off Slip-Ups. Aren't you glad you now know what *not* to do? Trust me, every one of the seven is well worth not doing!

WOMAN TILLS GARDEN with Teaspoon!

Now, I don't know about you, but I'm beginning to get tired of all this before-you-start-talking stuff. I feel like a preacher who's been going on so long even he's gotten tired of listening to the sermon. "Enough of the preliminaries, already, Stone. Let's get outside and turn some dirt!"

My sentiments, precisely. But — ahem — what are you going to turn that dirt with? Yes,

sad but true, you've just unearthed yet another groundbreaking topic: tools.

I'm going to make two general statements on that topic: one obvious; one perhaps a tad opinionated.

I tried to get away with using only the CHEAPEST garden implements — and ended up not implementing much in my garden!

Tool Truth #1: Good tools beat bad tools.

Tool Truth #2: Hand tools are better than power tools.

Tool Truth #1: Good tools are better than bad tools.

Thank you, thank you — yes, I know, I've really shared a revelation this time. But many of us ignore this simple truism for the simple reason that good tools *cost more* than bad tools.

They are worth it.

I bet every experienced gardener has a still-angry spot in his or her peaceful, plant-lover's heart for some poor-quality, shoddily made, unreliable, aggravating, downright *detestable* tool in his or her past. With me, it's hoses. I don't want to recall the number of kink-leaking, joint-spraying, sun-cracking, good-for-little hoses in my past. Some people talk to their plants? I talked to my hoses — and in no sweet terms. You see, I didn't learn my lesson when my first cheap hose performed, well, cheaply. No, the next year, I bought another. And the next year, another (it was a different color, so I figured it'd work better). Finally, four years ago, I went into the hardware store, said, "Give me the most expensive hose you've got," — and walked out a poorer but much happier man. The body of this high-quality hose was thicker, so it was less

likely to kink (or to crack when it did kink). Its ends were sturdier, so it was much less likely to leak. I haven't had any hose troubles since.

Now, I don't believe you have to purchase every garden implement and accessory under the sun. But, friends, when you do need to buy a garden tool, don't hold back. Get a good one.

Tool Truth #2: Hand tools are better than power tools.

Hand tools work at your pace. Power tools make you work at theirs. Hand tools connect

Tilled by Teaspoon

"It was my first garden. I didn't know you had to prepare the soil. I just went out there one day with a teaspoon, dug a few holes, and stuck some annuals in.

"And you know what? I was really surprised when they didn't grow!"
— *Kathleen Fisher, editor of* The American Gardener, *one of the most horticulturally sophisticated magazines in the country*

Rototiller Rampage

"While rear-tine tilling for the first time, a friend failed to lift the machine out of the soil at the end of the row, leading to one of the great chases in gardening history. She dug in her heels and was dragged 30 yards across the neighbors' lawn, leaving an 18-inch swath. Their lawn has never been quite the same!"
— *John Storey, President of Storey Communications*

you to your garden. Power tools separate you from it. Hand tools let you hear the world around you. Power tools drown out everything but their own racket.

I'm not a Luddite. I don't bicycle to work or wash my clothes in a creek. But come on — we're not doing our jobs or chores here, we're gardening. And one of the main purposes of gardening is to connect us to the earth, to help us relax and get more closely attuned to nature's rhythms. And I will admit to occasionally using a rototiller or gas-powered lawnmower (I'm not a glutton for toil), but I do so as sparingly as possible. There'll probably be times when you, too, will want to use a power tool in your garden. But the fewer the better. Chasing a noisy, strong, exhaust-spewing machine around a yard or garden is — let's admit it — not fun.

Corollary: Rent Power Tools, Don't Buy Them.

If you need to turn over a lot of dirt twice a year (spring and fall), rent that rototiller. If you really need to chop up brush only once a year, rent that chipper/shredder. And if you need to clean up fallen leaves only once a year, use a rake! (I'm sorry, I have no tolerance for leaf blowers.) If you eventually do decide to buy one of those yard machines, you'll have learned a lot more about it and your need for it *before* you spend all that money on it.

Counter Corollary: Don't Borrow Power Tools.

I don't know why, but Person A's tool in Person B's hands breaks 92.5 percent of the time. And then you've got two problems: you didn't finish the job you borrowed the tool for, and you've got yourself a sticky, potentially friendship-ending situation, to boot. I've been on both sides — lender and borrower — in this disaster, and it truly is a lose-lose situation. (I'm not going to tell you the sordid details of those sad stories. But I will say one thing: Keep a *close and constant eye* on the oil level of other people's power tools.)

Good and Bad Tools

OK, OK, enough with the generalities. Here are some specifics on the basic tools you will need.

Garden Fork

Garden fork

We're not talking here about a thin-tined pitch-fork for tossing loose (and light) hay down to the horses. Nope, you want a stout-pronged garden (or manure) fork for loosening soil, turning compost, breaking clods, mixing in compost, digging potatoes, dividing perennials — for getting things *done*. Get a sturdy one so the tines won't be likely to snap or the head break off the handle. And treat it with respect: don't use it as a crowbar to pry rocks or roots out of the soil. High quality or not, tines do break.

Shovel or Spade

The garden spade, a tool in vogue in the gardening catalogs these days, has a short handle with a D-shaped grip and a flat blade with a flat edge. Your basic shovel, on the other hand, is long handled with a curved blade and a curved digging edge. Some gardeners swear by the one, some by the other. Each is probably better for certain tasks: the flat cutting edge of the spade, for instance, makes it an ace at neatly slicing under sod you want to remove, while the long handle of the shovel makes it less back-straining for plain old digging. As far as I can determine, either one will work fine in a garden. Take your pick — that is, shovel or spade.

Garden Rake

This means one of those short-toothed, flat-headed (like a comb) sturdy steel rakes that can push dirt around, not a lightweight, fan-shaped leaf rake. It's especially good for shaping garden soil right before planting.

Trowel

For digging planting holes. Very handy (and very hard to keep track of).

Hoes

Which of the many, varied hand-weeding tools is best? Here we enter a place experienced gardeners frequently frequent: *The Land of Fervently Held Opinion.* People

Shovel

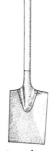

Spade

Trowel

swear by things that only look good holding shish kebab, as well as by monster tools that might moonlight at demolition sites. Well, here's the one I (and I'm not alone) swear by: **the stirrup hoe.** Also called the oscillating or scuffle hoe, it looks like a stirrup, but wiggles (oscillates) slightly as you use it.

God's gift to gardeners is what I'm really tempted to call it. Why? It's easy to use: you scuff it back and forth just under the surface of the soil. It cuts both ways, on both push and pull strokes. It slices weed roots right under the surface of the soil. And since it disturbs only the surface soil, it doesn't churn up the ground, which would bring a lot of unsprouted weed seeds to the surface.

Love's Labels Lost

"I always think — every year — I'll remember which seedlings I put in which cell pack, or that I'll recognize them when they come up. Guess what? I don't. (This comes from never stocking up on enough labels before the spring so I'll be able to write all the identifying tags I need.)

"My label problems don't stop there. After I put the plants, with proper I.D. markers, out in the garden, I soon find that the little plastic tags want to become dog toys. My two border collies love to tear the labels out and run around with them in their mouths. I have finally learned to combat this problem by burying each label in the mulch around the plant. That keeps the collies away, and keeps the labels from deteriorating in the sun."

— *Barbara Ellis, a freelance writer and editor in Alburtis, Pennsylvania*

Health Care for Tools

A fact of life: High-quality or low, tools won't last long if you don't care for them. Fortunately, garden hand tool care is not an overly demanding responsibility.

Put Them Away

Yes sir, this is the biggie! Find it, pick it up, put it back. Don't, don't, *don't* leave it out in the garden. The way weeds grow, you may never see it again. (If you're new to gardening, you may not realize that *I'm not kidding.*) Or you may see it again — when you rototill its handle or disinter it *next* spring. It really is amazing how much more slowly blades rust and handles rot if a tool is stored in a shed instead of left lying in the garden. (Does the fervor with which I state all this make you suspect Stone has *ever* left a tool of his own out? No, no, no . . .)

When you're putting an implement back, you may want to hose the dirt off the blade, spray a little lubricant on it, and rub some linseed oil into the handle. This would qualify you as "advanced" in the tool-care department and keep them "good as new" longer than most of us ever will be. If nothing else, it's certainly a good thing to do at the end of the season.

Sharpen Them

I think most people would rather wear themselves out hacking away with a dull tool than make their work easy by using a sharp one. Why? Because sharpening intimidates most of us. This is a mistake when it comes to garden tools because they are (a) a cinch to sharpen and (b) incredibly much easier to use

The secret to sharpening is to keep a constant angle.

afterward. We're not talking about some esoteric, highly advanced skill like honing a razor blade or (gasp) putting an edge on a pocket-knife here, folks. We're just trying to make those hoes and shovels slice into the dirt a bit more easily.

To do so, take a flat (also called bastard) file and rub it at an angle against the cutting edge of the tool's blade. Which is the cutting edge? Look at the blade. It's the side that isn't flat. Should you push the file into the blade or down the blade? Far as I can tell, some folks do one, some the other. What angle should you file at? Try to copy the one that's already there. How long should you do it? Until a thin band along the edge looks shiny and the tip feels sharp when you gently rub a finger over the edge. (A dull edge feels smooth, a sharp edge sort of "snags" your finger.)

Sound simple? It is. There's really only one trick to watch out for: *Try to be consistent.* Hold the file at the same angle the whole time you work. If you "round" the file as you push or pull, you'll be rounding, not pointing, the edge as well.

Do sharpen your hand tools. You will be amazed how much better they work. It's one of the great labor-saving secrets of gardening.

The stirrup hoe has only one limitation: it doesn't work well on large weeds. (On the other hand, it's so easy to use, I truly don't have near as many large weeds to hoe as I used to.) For large weeds

Stirrup hoe

you need a hoe with more heft, something that can really chop at those leafy undesirables. As far as I'm concerned, the standard broad-faced hardware-store hoe works fine. However, you may come up with a favorite heavy-hoeing tool of your own.

Wheelbarrow or Garden Cart

For lugging compost, hauling weeds, pulling mulch, and other moving needs — here's another plain, basic, multipurpose garden tool. Carts are more stable, since they have two wheels, but they're also more expensive. Get whichever you prefer, as long as it's of good quality.

A Good Hose

I already told you what happens to cheapskates (like me) who buy cheap hoses. If you live in a dry area, you'll probably find a drip-irrigation set worth all the coin and complexity it entails. Why? Because drip systems use only around one third as much water as hoses do, and they deliver it right where plants need it — at their roots.

I'm not going to get much into drip irrigation here: it's a big topic, and we'll dive into it in Chapter 10. There are two basic types — **soaker hoses** that drip water all along their length, and **emitter systems** that drip only at carefully placed doodads called (you guessed it) emitters. Both work best buried under the surface of soil or mulch in fairly permanent locations: with perennial flower beds or under fruit trees, for instance. However, I do have one soaker hose that's not "installed" underground. I move this one around from row to row in my vegetable garden during dry spells.

■ ■ ■ ■ ■

There's a world of other garden aids and implements you can buy. Most are not essential; many you can acquire as you need them. But the basic ones here should be enough to get you started.

FIENDISH PLOT Overturned!

At last! The weather's clear! Spring is here! Time to quit schooling and start tooling! (No fooling!) Yes, yes, it's finally time to break ground on that new garden!

Not!

Well, maybe not. You see, there are three basic groundbreaking goofs people often make. Indeed, so many gardeners have made these slip-ups that I'm tempted to call them **Classic Gardening Mistakes.** And **Classic Mistake #1,** appropriately, comes from being too eager to start turning turf.

I turned my garden when it was too wet — and it turned on me!

I know you're eager. You may have been waiting every weekend for weeks while April showers have been doing their May-flower thing. But just because *this* Saturday turns out to be the first sunny Saturday since the invention of the Roman calendar doesn't necessarily mean it's the right day to prepare the garden.

Here's the problem. If you try to turn the ground when the soil's too *wet*, the soil won't break down into those fine little pieces baby plant roots love to snuggle up against, but instead will clump together in big, wet lumps that eventually dry out into brick-hard boulders of dirt.

Conversely, try to work it when the ground's too *dry* and — unless you're gardening in sand — it just won't work at all. It will be so hard and solid that you'll be waging a losing, or at least very laborious, battle.

Does that first possibility sound a tad, say, exaggerated, like nagging, overprotective, listen-to-your-garden-book talk? OK, don't be-

Night of the Living Weeds

"How about half of a solution? I read somewhere that you could leave pulled weeds right in the garden for mulch. That sounded good to me. But here in western North Carolina, it's likely to rain the day after you weed. So guess what? All the plants you pulled and left in the garden will start growing right back up again!"

— *Annie Ager, a wonderful neighbor of the author's in Fairview, North Carolina*

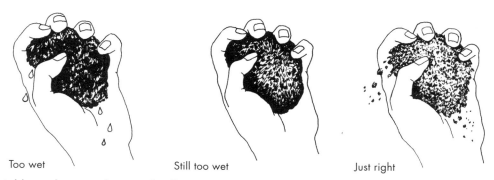

| Too wet | Still too wet | Just right |

The highly sophisticated, scientifically precise (OK, maybe not, but it works) soil moisture test

lieve me. Go ahead and work your garden when it's too wet. Lots of gardeners do . . . *once.*

Testing Soil Moisture

How do you tell if the soil's too wet to till? Grab a handful and squeeze. Does water drip out? It's definitely too wet. Does it compress into a ball and stay that way? Still too wet. Does it crumble in your hand? You're ready to go! (Alternatively, you can *drop* that handful and see if it falls apart. If it does, go to it.)

How do you tell if the soil's too *dry* to work? If it's hard. Push a spade into the earth. If that ground is solid and bricklike, you'll be doing yourself a big favor if you water it thoroughly today and start working it a day or two later.

Tilling

OK, the weather's fine and the ground, like the little bear's porridge, is just right. Let's get to work. Assuming you're starting a new garden where lawn or pasture has been growing, you're ready to face **Classic Mistake #2:**

I plowed sod and planted seeds. I got bugs and I got weeds!

The surface of your new garden is covered with sod, a matted layer of plants (mostly grasses) and roots. Now, you *could* get a tractor or a rototiller (a mighty strong rototiller) to turn and mix all that sod into the soil. And it's not fatal if you do so. But then all those grass rhizomes (including hard-to-beat species like witchgrass and quackgrass) will be eager to resprout. All the tough-rooted weeds, like dandelion, burdock, and thistle, will still fight for their share of the sun. All the grubs, cutworms, and various other insect pupae will be looking for some plantlets to munch on and, not finding the ones that used to be there, will settle for the ones you put there.

Better off you are (as our old chum Yoda, the Jedi Master, would say) to **remove that sod completely and then turn the dirt.** And the best tool for this job is a spade (the digging tool with the straight, flat edge, remember?). However, a shovel (the scoop-faced one) will serve if you're spadeless.

Removing the Sod

To commence, mark out your garden area with stakes and string. Start at one side, slice the spade into the ground, and then push it almost horizontally to cut under the sod roots. If you have a partner, that person can grab the cut sod edge and peel it up as you cut underneath — in fact, rolling it up as you go like carpet. (You can slice the sides of this "roll" as needed to make it come up easier.)

If you're on your own, cut out squares of sod and load them into a wheelbarrow. What do you do with all this rolled or square-cut sod? The best use is patching thin spots in your lawn. Dig up poor-looking areas, set down sections of healthy sod, and water it well. (And keep it watered — when needed — for the next three or four weeks.) If your lawn doesn't need any Band-Aids, compost the sod. Stack it, upside down, in a big pile. Turn the pile after a month or two if you want to speed up decomposition, or just leave it and wait a year. You'll end up with a mound of good soil-building organic matter you can add to your young garden.

Once you've shaved your site bald, you can then rent a rototiller or get down to digging. Renting? The rule here is **the bigger, the better.** Try to get one of those big, way-too-heavy-to-lift, rear-tine tillers. Don't expect one of those cute little wheelless cultivators to be able to break new ground. Similarly, don't expect a front-tine tiller (the kind with the ground-chopping blades in front of the engine) to do the job easily or comfortably. Even with

And Be Careful with the Ashes

"One of my first gardens was in rural Pennsylvania. After a neighboring farmer plowed up the place for our plot, we made a homemade harrow, sort of a protruding fin, that we dragged over and over through the garden, making the soil as fine as we possibly could.

"The only problem was that the site was full of quackgrass. All our harrowing had cut the quackgrass into hundreds and hundreds of tiny little pieces, and every single one grew a new plant!

"One neighbor we told about it said that the only way to get rid of quackgrass is to pull out all the roots and burn them. 'And then,' he added, 'you better be darned careful what you do with the ashes.'"

— *Sara Pitzer of Richfield, North Carolina, author of* **Buying and Selling Antiques**

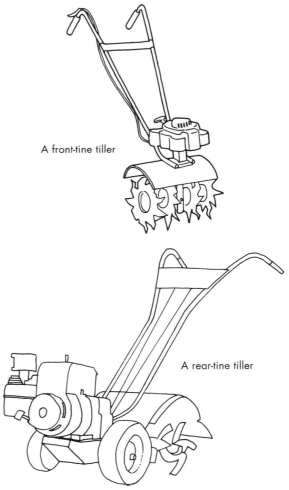

A front-tine tiller

A rear-tine tiller

When it comes to tillers, biggest is bestest.

a big rear-tine tiller, understand that you're going to be working. The job will take several passes on each row (and making those 180° turns at the ends of rows is real sport!).

Digging? **The longer the handle, the better.** You'll do less bending. Either a shovel or spade will work fine for the initial turning; then a good garden fork will help you toss, crumble, smack, and otherwise turn big clods into small ones. Taking sideways, hands-spread swipes at clumps with a garden fork, as if you were *trying* to make golf divots with a baseball bat, is one way to break up clumps. It's called "tilthing"; it gives your garden good texture, or "tilth"!

When you've got the soil loose and crumbly ("friable" in gardener's lingo), you'd be smart to sift it. Build a wooden frame to support a section of half-inch hardware screen, set it over your wheelbarrow, and actually *sift* the topsoil in your new growing area, bucket by bucket, to get out the remaining roots, rhizomes, and insect pests. Laborious? Yes, indeed, but compared to the job you'll have later trying to control weeds and pests if you don't take this extra step, it's actually time saving.

Of course, working the soil up isn't the whole job. You'll want to fertilize it, and you'll want to start improving ("building") it. I'll be covering fertilizing in the next chapter. I know, I probably should have gone over it before we broke ground, but, come on — I was as eager as you to get started! Still, there are some basic soil-improving steps you can take right now while you're shaping up your plot.

Raised Beds

One of the best is to make **raised beds** in your garden, 3- to 4-foot-wide growing strips separated by 2-foot (more or less) pathways. Raised beds have a host of virtues. They warm

"Tilthing" soil with a garden fork is like making golf divots on purpose!

Carrots with an 'L'

When I went to harvest my carrots, they were L-shaped! I hadn't tilled deep enough, and they took the easiest route — sideways!

Kathleen M. Billings, receptionist and administrative assistant at Storey Publishing

Work now, not later: sift the soil of a new garden.

up more quickly in spring. They drain water better in wet times or damp locations. They keep the soil from getting compressed around your plants (because you always step in the pathways and never on the beds). In addition, since so little space is used on pathways, they allow you to grow more crops in the same area.

Best of all for new gardens, raised beds allow you to concentrate your soil-improving efforts. (Why waste precious compost or fertilizer on paths?) The worse your soil is initially, the more this virtue can come into play. Maybe, for instance, all the topsoil was scraped off during the construction of your home, so your new plot is nothing but clay subsoil. Faced with that situation, some growers don't even *try* to prepare their subsoil, but, in effect, help it end up back where it belongs. They build raised-bed frames on top of it, fill the frames with hauled-in topsoil, and just garden in that.

How do you make raised beds? There are several ways. You can build wooden frames from boards nailed together either horizontally or vertically. (By the way, you *could* use pressure-treated wood to build the beds — it's not *supposed* to leach its toxic preservatives into the soil — but I wouldn't risk it myself, at least not on food crops. I'd rather just replace the lumber when it rots.) You can prepare raised beds every spring by first tilling or digging all the garden soil and then simply shoveling the loose pathway soil right into the bed areas and raking it smooth. (Some rototillers have furrowing attachments that will mechanically push soil out of your pathways.) Or you can go the whole-hog, true-dedication route and **doubledig** your beds.

Doubledigging

Doubledigging, best espoused by John Jeavons in his important book *How to Grow More Vegetables* (Ten Speed Press), is part of the ultimate space-saving, fertility-building gardening method. Indeed, Jeavons has refined his "biointensive" techniques to give four times the yields of conventional agriculture.

The basic concept behind doubledigging is that plants will do better if their roots have plenty of loose soil in which to grow. Well, this method provides plenty of root room — it loosens the earth up to 2 feet deep! In contrast, a tiller will loosen only 4 to 6 inches; and a good hand-digging job, 8 to 12 inches.

The technique is simple, but it does take work. Dig a 12-inch-deep, spade-wide trench *across* your garden bed, removing all the dirt and putting it in a wheelbarrow. Then repeatedly jam a garden fork into that trench and shift it back and forth, to loosen that lower soil as much as possible. Next, get out of the trench (you don't want to compress that subsoil) and dig a new trench right next to it, throwing the dirt from trench two into trench one. After that, stand in trench two and loosen its subsoil well with a garden fork.

You've got the routine by now, right? Next,

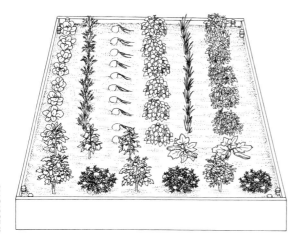

A wooden frame raised bed lets you concentrate your soil-building efforts where plants will grow.

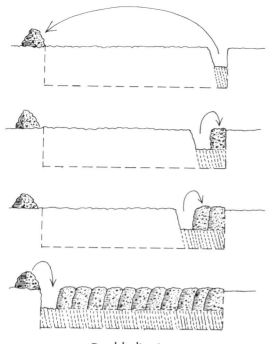

Doubledigging:
maximum work, maximum results

you dig trench three, throwing its dirt in trench two, loosen its subsoil, and start trench four. You repeat the procedure until you get to the end of the garden, where you'll end up with an empty, loosened trench but no soil (from a new row) to fill it with. Where will you find some? Look in your wheelbarrow. The dirt from the very first trench you made gets to fill the trench on its opposite end. By the time you're done spading, you'll have a raised bed — all that digging and loosening raises the surface of the soil — with a very-well-loosened base.

One Final Dig

Weeds never wait, but I did — and then I didn't rework the soil before planting.

OK, using your method of choice, you've thoroughly worked up your soil, you've fertil- ized it (as will be described in the next chapter), and you're ready to plant. If you're a speed gardener and have done all this in one day, grow to it. But if there's going to be some waiting time, even just a week, between your initial ground preparation and some of your planting, it's time to bring up **Classic Mistake #3**.

Garden soil is full of weed seeds. Lots of weed seeds. Thousands of weed seeds. Start thinking them as frisky fifth graders just waiting for the "school's out" bell to ring. Anytime you turn garden soil, you bring hundreds of weed seeds up to the surface, ready and eager — very eager! — to break out. Even if you don't see any popping through the surface yet, they're swelling and sprouting underground.

Don't ever let those weeds get a head start on your plants. Always rework the surface of your garden *right before* you plant. Till it, fork it, or (my preference) work it over once with a stirrup hoe. In fact, if you can, prepare the soil a few weeks before you're going to plant; then, once a week, rework the surface. That will help knock back a few generations of weed seeds.

■ ■ ■ ■ ■

Besides, you're not ready to plant yet, anyway. You've got to read the next chapter first, remember?

To Dig or Not to Dig

A minority of gardeners don't dig, till, spade, fork, or hoe their gardens at all. They *bury* them — with mulch.

They cover their gardens with lots and lots and lots of organic matter: newspaper, hay, leaves, compost, cardboard. If they're starting a garden on sod, they smother that sod with the mulch for a year, killing and decomposing it. The second year, they plant.

How do you plant through mulch? Pull it back enough to stick transplants in or open a line through it for row crops.

Mulching imitates nature. It keeps the soil moist. It adds fertility where it's most needed, near the surface. It boosts the organic matter of the soil. It encourages earthworms, nature's natural soil builders. (Do you think earthworms appreciate being roughed up by rototillers?) It keeps soil cool in hot weather. It smothers weeds.

Drawbacks? Most are minor. Mulched soil warms more slowly in the spring, so you can't get as early a start on heat-loving crops (unless you pull it back from those sections for a few weeks). Heavy mulching isn't the most space-saving method, something to consider if you're pinched for room. Mulch also gives slugs and snails plenty of cool, damp places to live.

The biggest factor to consider if you want to try being a deep-mulch gardener is the mulch itself: you're going to need a *lot* of it. I tried mulching a large section of my garden last spring, spreading a lot (twenty-seven bales!) of old hay over my soil. Everything looked neat, trim, and well covered in May. By August, weeds had sprouted in the cracks, like trees in sidewalks. Others had shot up in all the too-thin spots. And more were waiting in line for any new opportunities.

Mulch needs periodic replenishing because it keeps breaking down (that's one of its virtues, remember?). So you'll need to locate and haul and spread a lot of natural material if you want to go this route. If you can do that, you may do well to consider "going mulch."

READER SKIPS Chapter 5! Plants All Die!

Dear reader, I have a writer's — not a gardener's — confession to make. I put off covering this chapter's topic because, well, I'm not really excited about soil fertility. I mean, who wants to talk about it? Gardening's about growing plants, about tumescent tomatoes and adorable asters. It's not a reprise of high school chemistry, for Pete's sake!

Well, that, friends, is the biggest mistake you can make with this chapter: ignoring it. Simply because you, too, might not be overstimulated by a discussion of potential hydrogen or leachable nitrates does not mean you can get away with avoiding it. (No, no, no!) Just digging up some soil and plopping in some plants will not lead to a very successful garden experience (unless, lucky beginner, your ground is already in well-balanced, well-fertilized shape). You will need to know and deal with some basic aspects of soil fertility to get good results from gardening.

Thank goodness, you don't have to go to the opposite extreme and become an expert on the topic, either. You can grow wonderful gardens without ever learning the difference between an anion and an actinomycete. Just get hold of the basics, give them a moderate amount of attention, and you'll be fine.

I'll help you take care of the first part of that here. The lesson won't be too hard to absorb, either, because the main ingredient we'll be using is common sense. In fact, although this chapter is going to go through a bit of chemical rigamarole, if you wanted to sum it all up in the simplest form possible, the lesson would be this:

1. Take a soil test
2. Fix the pH
3. Add the appropriate fertilizers

The pH pHactor

I haven't improved my soil's fertility because chemistry intimidates me and always has!

This is both the easiest and the most important fertility factor to deal with in your garden. To the soil scientist, pH means "potential

An actinomycete?

An anion?

What's the difference? Don't worry about it!

hydrogen" and is a way of measuring how many hydrogen ions are in the soil. If that sounds a bit technical, just think of it the way the old-timers did: how sweet or sour is your soil? (Many of them could actually tell by tasting it.)

Potential hydrogen is measured on a scale of 1 (most acid) to 14 (most alkaline), with 7 being neutral. The scale is logarithmic, which means each number is ten times higher or lower than the previous one. Thus, a soil with a pH of 5 would be ten times more acidic than one with a pH of 6, and one hundred times more acidic than one with a pH of 7.

Why is pH important? The vast majority of garden plants will not do well if the pH is too far off from neutral because **extremely acid or alkaline soil ties up essential nutrients,** keeping them from being absorbed by plants. In other words, you can add all the fertilizer in the world to your garden, but if it's too acid or too alkaline, things won't grow — or at least won't grow well.

THE pH SCALE

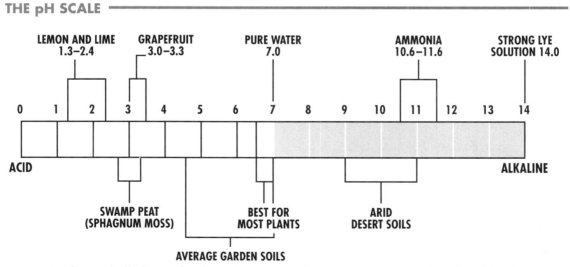

Acidity and alkalinity of soils and common substances, as measured by the pH scale.
Most plants prefer their soil to be neutral or slightly acidic (between 6.5 and 7.0).

The vast majority of garden plants prefer their soil close to neutral, maybe just a tad on the acid side: a pH between 6.5 and 7.0.

Some plants (like blueberries, azaleas, and rhododendrons) love more acidic conditions, and some are alkaline lovers (like lilacs, sweet peas, and asparagus), but they are the exceptions. Near neutral is the rule.

Fortunately, pH is easy to deal with. First off, take a soil sample from your garden. Second, either test it yourself with a do-it-yourself kit or send it off to a testing service. And third, add the appropriate amendment to your soil, if needed, to raise or lower your pH to the proper level.

Step One: Taking a Soil Sample

To take a soil sample, dig a 6-inch hole in your garden. Then scrape out a ½-inch-thick slice all the way down the side of the hole. Repeat in several different locations around your garden.

Mix all these samples together. Take a pint's worth of the mix, spread it out on something to dry in the sun, and then put it in a plastic bag.

To keep from skewing the results, use clean tools and containers for this job, touch the soil as little as possible, and don't (obviously) draw your sample from spots where you've recently spread fertilizer.

Step Two: Testing Your Soil

Soil test kits are widely available at garden centers. The cheap ones aren't really very accurate at nutrient analysis (I wouldn't rely on them), but they can do an OK job of checking pH. Your county agricultural extension service should offer inexpensive testing, or you can hunt down a private testing lab. Country or private labs give the

Eliot's Weird-Thinking Story

"To me, solving problems in biological agriculture is often a case of punting; that is, putting on your imagination cap and trying to figure out something that may work. As an example, one time I noticed that seaweed was a great fertilizer for potatoes, a crop originally grown in the mountains, but lousy for cabbage, a coastal crop. That led me to trying the opposite tack, putting composted hardwood leaves — a 'mountain fertilizer' — on cabbage plantings. Sure enough, it worked just great.

"One year I needed to do a really good job with my tomato crop and was puzzling over what organic fertilizer would be best, when a nearby farmer offered me a load of fresh pig manure. Aha, I thought, in my best weird-thinking mode, pigs are round and pink. So are tomatoes. A perfect match!

"I dumped all that fresh pig plop on my beds — and ended up with the worst tomato crop I've ever had. The vines started getting blight in May!

"That's definitely my most poorly solved horticultural problem. Now whenever I suddenly come up with a great idea for some problem I'm facing, I always stop myself and ask, 'Is this going to be another pig [bleep] solution?'"

— Eliot Coleman, Maine grower and author of the excellent The New Organic Grower

most accurate results, but it can take a while to get results — and, in spring, who wants to wait? (Hint: fall is the best time to take your soil test for next year.)

Step Three: Correcting the pH

Once you have your pH result, you can get to work. In the eastern U.S., your soil is likely to be **too acid.** Most people use ground limestone to fix that. Dolomitic lime is better than calcic lime because most gardens need the magnesium in the former more than the extra calcium in the latter.

The numbers: if you have sandy soil, 5 pounds of limestone per 100 square feet of garden should be enough to raise the pH one point. If you have loamy soil, 10 pounds per 100 square feet should do the job. And if you have clay soil, 12 to 15 pounds per 100 square feet

will be needed. Spread the powder by hand, going over your garden once in one direction and then again at right angles. Work the powder into the soil either by hand or by machine.

If your soil's **too alkaline** (common in the Southwest), the most common cure is gypsum (calcium sulfate). In most soils, 2 pounds per 100 square feet should lower the pH a point. However, gypsum contains calcium, which most alkaline soils already have in abundance. So a better way to drop that pH one point might be to work in one inch of peat moss.

Acid or alkaline, if your soil pH needs a lot of adjusting, don't try to change it more than one point a year. Too abrupt a change in pH is not good for the microbial soil life.

That's about it for pH. Check it annually the first two or three years you garden, then only once every few years after that.

The Big Three: nitrogen, phosphorus, and potassium

The Big Three

Let's move on to the actual physical ingredients of plants. Actually, the three biggest components of plants are carbon, hydrogen, and oxygen, but you don't need to worry about these. Plants get all the C, H, and O they need from air and water.

There are, however, three major mineral nutrients you do need to be concerned with: **nitrogen** (N), **phosphorus** (P), and **potassium** (K), which is also called potash. In oversimplified terms, nitrogen builds leaves, phosphorus builds fruits, and potassium builds roots.

These three nutrients are so important, almost all garden-store fertilizer bags have three numbers on them to point out their NPK percentage. For instance, a fertilizer marked 5-10-10 has 5 percent nitrogen, 10 percent phosphorus, and 10 percent potassium.

Chemical vs. Organic Fertilizers

Should you use chemical or organic fertilizers in your garden? I'm an organic gardener myself, so I use organic ones. They tend to be longer lasting and less likely to wash away in rain. A good organic fertilizer also contains organic matter to help build up your soil's overall quality. Chemical fertilizers are generally faster acting. You might say they're like vitamins: good for correcting a short-term deficiency, but not best for overall health. If you ate a junk-food-and-vitamin diet, you could get the same major-mineral content in your body as someone who ate a more wholesome diet based on grains, vegetables, and fruits. But the fiber and many minor nutrients of the latter diet would obviously make it more healthful in the long run.

So I'd say if you want to use some chemical

Don't overdo it.

fertilizers to help correct initial deficiencies in your garden right away, well . . . OK. In the long run, though, your garden will do best if you work on building up its overall health (in ways we'll cover, don't worry).

I overfertilized, thinking that if a little fertilizer was good, more would be even better!

One word of warning: Don't overdo it. This, I bet you could guess, is The Great Mistake of Fertilizing. Too much fertilizer can actually have all sorts of harmful side effects, from "burning" plants (injuring their leaf tissues) to attracting insect pests.

Nitrogen

This is a tricky one because although nitrogen gas makes up more than three-quarters of our atmosphere, gaseous nitrogen is unusable by plants. They need mineral nitrogen — nitrates or ammonia — which are both readily used up by plants and, worse yet, water soluble.

Indeed, because nitrogen levels can fluctuate widely in the soil, many soil labs won't give you an N reading at all.

Plants need a lot of nitrogen, though, so you'll continually have to keep supplying it to your soil. Sadly, most fertilizers, chemical or natural, provide all their nitrogen at once. That sort of "use it or lose it" approach can create feast-then-famine conditions. The best way to give your ground an ongoing supply of nitrogen is to add organic matter to your soil regularly because that will slowly release the element as it breaks down.

There's a hitch here, though: fresh organic matter actually absorbs some nitrogen during its initial breakdown; as it decomposes further, it releases the nitrogen it absorbed and more. This means you should add aged organic matter (such as compost) to your soil or, if you do add fresh green matter, wait a few weeks before you plant. (We'll get into all that in a bit.)

For an initial supply of nitrogen, you could use a chemical fertilizer or an organic one such as blood meal (14 percent N), fish meal (10 percent N), cottonseed meal (8 percent N), chicken manure (4–6 percent N), or animal manure (2–4 percent N). It's impossible for me to tell you how much you need, but generally around 1 pound of a 10 percent N fertilizer per 100 square feet should be a reasonably safe bet. (Adjust to suit your fertilizer of choice: ergo, 2 pounds of a 5 percent N fertilizer, 2.5 pounds of a 4 percent one, etc.)

Remember, don't add too much. Nitrogen-heavy plants often develop lots of foliage but have trouble flowering and fruiting. They also seem particularly tasty to the bad bugs of the world. (Conversely, a lot of yellowed leaves may be a sign of nitrogen deficiency.)

Pests like lots of nitrogen.

Well, that's enough about nitrogen. Thank goodness the other nutrients are much simpler to deal with.

Phosphorus

A good soil test will give you a phosphorus rating. You can then buy an appropriate fertilizer and amend your soil as needed. Some good organic sources of phosphorus are bonemeal (24–28 percent P), colloidal phosphate (20 percent P) and single superphosphate (20 percent P). Finely ground phosphate rock (30 percent P) is slow-releasing, so it's best thought of as a long-term phosphorus source.

Potassium

Mr. K is an equally straightforward soil-building ingredient. Just use your soil test to

Black Rubber

"When I left my dad's nursery and started working at a little nursery in Canoga Park, California, I didn't really know much about caring for dryland plants. One day I wanted to feed some plants, so I simply broadcast granular fertilizer in all the plant containers.

"In a few days, all the leaves on the nursery's six big rubber plants turned black and fell off. The trees were completely bare! They eventually recovered, but that experience taught me a lesson: never feed a 'dry' plant."

— *Lili Singer, editor of*
The Southern California Gardener

figure out how much you need. Some organic sources of potash are kelp meal (3 percent K), greensand (7 percent K), crushed granite (4 percent K). wood ashes (8 percent K), and sulpo-mag (22 percent K).

The Little Ten

At least ten other mineral nutrients are crucial for plant growth. The three "major minors" (most needed of the others) are **calcium, sulphur,** and **magnesium.** The first two are generally abundant in most soils. The third, magnesium (often reported on soil tests), is an ingredient of dolomitic limestone and raw rock phosphate.

The "minor minors" are **boron, chlorine, copper, iron, manganese, molybdenum,** and

Straw Ain't Hay

"When I first learned about mulch — I was reading Ruth Stout's books, I guess — I was so excited I got hold of some alfalfa hay and put it all over my vegetable garden. Now, I didn't know then that hay has seeds and straw does not. Sure enough, before long all that alfalfa sprouted. I was weeding it out of my garden for years to come. Oh, well, at least it was easy to pull — and it taught me the difference between straw and hay!"

— Kathleen Yeomans, author of
The Able Gardener

zinc. The basic soil-building practices I keep hinting about (and will, indeed, get to) should eventually take care of these trace mineral needs. For now, 1 pound of kelp (seaweed) per 100 square feet of garden should provide a useful initial supply of them.

■ ■ ■ ■ ■

Well, friends, that's about long enough in the chemistry classroom, don't you agree? Let me end our session here by telling you that you can avoid ever having to enter this room again. That's right, there's a secret for never again (after your initial fertilization) having to worry about pH, nitrogen, trace minerals — the whole garden-chemical stew!

Start and maintain an ongoing soil-building program — in effect, work at growing soil as well as plants.

How do you do that? Gee, I'm glad you asked. It's a fascinating topic and just may be the key to gardening success.

But . . . it does involve another session in the classroom, albeit biology class instead of chemistry class. And I don't know about you, but I need a break from textbook gardening. Our soil's ready to plant. So let's get out in the dirt. We can come back to this soil-building topic after we've got things growing.

For now, though, let's have some fun playing with seeds!

---
6. READY, SET, SOW!

GARDENERS REGRET: "If Only We Had Labeled!"

Yes, it's planting time! The earth is ready, the season is far enough along, you've made it through Soil Chem 101 — it's get out and grow time! Sow, team, sow!

Planting seeds really does merit such enthusiasm. This primordial act of agriculture springs from an impulse deep in our nature. Indeed, the combination of hand, soil, and seed casts a spell on every grower, new and old. This annual ritual of newness, the season, and life never, ever fails to stir a gardener's blood.

And guess what? Sowing seeds is easy. There aren't a whole lot of ways to mess up on this. Well, OK, there are some — and I'll cover them. But, basically, here's something sweet and simple.

Let's do it. Got your tools? You'll need a hoe, some stakes, string (optional), pen and paper, and, of course, seeds. Your soil should be fertilized and worked up so that it has "good tilth" (that's garden talk for "no big lumps"). You've recently (better yet, *just*) hoed the surface one last time — even if you didn't see any weeds sprouting — to make sure no weeds are

The highly complex tools of seed sowing

about to sprout and get a head start on the seeds you're going to sow. It's time to say . . .

Ready? Set? Sow!

To begin, stick a stake in the ground at one end of your planting row and another at the other

The seed trench: An
easy row to hoe

end. Then, walking backward between the two, use a corner of your hoe to make a small trench from one stake to the other. If you want to make sure your row is straight, tie some string between the two stakes before you start trenching to guide your ditching efforts.

Sowing Rules of Thumb

How deep should you make your trench? The rule of thumb is: **bury seeds at a depth three times their diameter** — in other words, not very deep. A fat bean seed is about ⅜ of an inch. Three times that is only 1⅛ inch. A tiny lettuce seed isn't even ¹⁄₁₆ of an

inch across; three times that is less than ¼ of an inch!

But don't fret about such measurements! The point here is simply this: seeds don't need to be set very deep. The natural human tendency is to stick them down, way down, in the ground. So that "three times" rule is really just a reminder that you're trying to *plant* your seeds, not *bury* them. Don't worry about fractions of an inch; the little things are quite eager to get their leaves out of the ground. Just use that rule as a reminder not to inter your sowings.

How thickly should you sow? **The bigger the seeds, the farther apart they can go.** Your seed packets may well have suggestions, saying things like space corn seeds 4 to 6 inches apart, and melon seeds in hills 2 to 3 feet apart. Or they may cop out and say "plant evenly." Now, *that's* useful!

I'd suggest this: think about how far apart you want the mature plants to be — and then plant your seeds twice as close as that. Why? Because not all seeds germinate (not for me, anyway). So I'd rather oversow an area and thin out overcrowded sprouts later than risk undersowing it and have big gaps in my garden. (Very *tiny* seeds, though, are very hard to keep from oversowing. Some gardeners will mix them with sand to thin them and sprinkle that in the row.)

Don't cover the row yet — the open trench can help you site your next row. Pace off the distance to the new row at both ends of the first one (a recommended distance between rows *will* be on your seed packet), set two more stakes and repeat the process. Once all the rows for this crop are dug and planted, use your hoe to cover your seeds and to lightly tamp the soil down on top of them.

Row spacing is kind of variable, really, and depends on three factors: **soil fertility,** weeding, and access. The more fertile your soil, the closer you can have plants grow. Most seed packet recommendations are on the "give them lots of room" end of the spectrum, and that's probably the safe way to go at first. You'll get a better feel for how close you can plant as you gain experience. One obvious sign: if the plants don't get as big as you'd hoped, you may have stuck them too close together. For instance, I never put broccoli plants closer than 18 inches apart any more because I got smaller heads when I did.

The weeding factor has to do with how you intend to keep those inevitable intruders under control. If you're going to rototill between the rows, you'll want them separated by the width of your tiller and then some (both for margin of error and to keep from tearing up any crop plant roots). If you're going to hand hoe or

mulch to keep weeds down, then the closer the rows, the less work for you.

Access? Well, tiny seeds turn into big plants, and you need to have room between rows to get to them — or else how are you going to tend and harvest them? So allow enough room for you to still get in after the leaves poke out into the aisles.

And Sow On: Beds and Broadcasting

We'd also better discuss two variations on the classic "Ye Olde Rowes and Stringe" sowing pattern: beds and broadcasting. Remember our discussion about gardening in beds from way back in the very first chapter? (You can refresh your memory by looking back — it's allowed — if need be.) If you decide to garden in beds, you don't have to worry about getting yourself between the plant rows anymore: just reach in there from the sides of the bed. You can even use an extra space-saving trick and plant in hexagons. This pattern (which you can also visualize as staggered rows) fits more plants in an area while still preserving the correct distance between them. I'd definitely recommend it for bed gardeners.

Lots of gardeners don't plant leaf crops (lettuce, spinach, Swiss chard, kale, and the like) in rows, but broadcast them by hand over an area. It's fun — just sprinkle the seeds around the area as evenly as you can, first in one direction, then in the other at right angles to the first. Lightly rake over the area to cover the seeds. (In my area, an old mountain gardener I knew — who grew only leafy greens — used to go to his plot just before a May rainstorm, throw all his seeds about, come back in, and say, "There! I've planted the garden." It worked.) Don't make the area too wide; you need to be able to reach into the middle of it for thinning, weeding, and harvesting.

Tag Time

I UPROOTED precious seedlings because I didn't know what they were! I PAMPERED invasive weeds because I thought I did know what they were.

"Out of sight, out of mind," the old proverb goes. In gardening, it's "Out of sight — *what is it?!*" You must identify your sowings, by both plant and variety, as soon as you cover that seed. Fail not to do this; it has to be the most obvious oversight (i.e., mistake) of seed sowing.

Now, the old gardener's trick here is just to turn that empty seed packet over on top of one of your stakes and leave it there. That simple strategy doesn't work for me; the paper packets always wash away, blow away, hitch a ride with a passing bird, or somehow or other disappear. Many gardeners write plant names down with an indelible marker on flat sticks or purchased plant-identification labels. That's a better method.

Personally, though, since the weeds of chaos are always creeping in around the edges of my life — and garden — I don't trust labels alone. I also make a diagram on paper, showing where, what, and when I planted something. Then I post that someplace that I can actually *remember* where it is. (No point in having a planting diagram if you can't find it, I have discovered.) Having a backup system like this or recording the information in a garden journal is a good practice to follow. (Trust me.)

Water Well and Regularly

An empty pot never boils and a dry seed never sprouts.

A seed without water will not germinate — ever. A seedling that runs out of water will die — always. Therefore, if you want a seed to grow, you must **keep it constantly moist** — that's *constantly,* as in steadily, regularly, invariably, unwaveringly, downright unintermittently. So water your newly planted rows well as soon as you plant them. And *anytime* the soil surface *starts* to dry out, water it again.

This is especially important with tiny-seeded crops, perhaps because they're close to the surface. (Big seeds often seem to be reliable germinators.) Then, too, some plants are naturally slower to germinate than others. When you plant a tiny-seeded slow starter, well, you've *definitely* got your watering work cut out for you.

Indeed, in situations like that, some gardeners — me, for instance — resort to sneaky

---

Carrot Seed Regatta

"I used to plant carrots as early as possible. That means January or February here in Santa Barbara, California. That's our rainy season, and carrots need a lot of moisture to germinate, but for a really long time, I wasn't getting any carrot sprouts at all.

"I had no idea why . . . until one day I went out after a good storm and noticed all my carrot seeds floating away down the path! Now I cover my carrot seeds with floating row covers or even turned-over flats until they start to sprout."

— Kathleen Yeomans, author of
The Able Gardener

tricks. For example, I cover my newly sown and watered carrot bed with *plywood* to keep it from drying out. After about five days, I'll look under the wood every morning. When I finally see lines of needle-thin leaf pairs starting to come up where I sowed carrot seed, I'll take the boards off right away so the sprouts won't die from lack of light.

Water Deep

I'm not a shallow person, but, yes, I was a shallow waterer.

Watering well does not mean soaking a spot with the hose until it starts to puddle. That may seem like you're flooding a spot, but if you stop then, you're probably *under*watering it. Don't

The Year of the Sunflower Genocide

"Most of our garden disaster stories turn out to be very hackneyed, involving neglect and weeds, the world's most common gardening sins.

"We did have the Year of the Sunflower Genocide, which was sort of brainlessly disastrous. We have this nice little notebook with a picture of a cow on the front in which (theoretically) we keep seed lists and maps of each year's garden, so we'll know where we planted what and what happened. In practice, however, unable to locate the little book, we go dashing out every spring and, in a burst of mass enthusiasm, all madly plant things at once, insisting as we go along that we remember exactly what we're doing, which we don't. (We do stick little stakes in the ground to mark the rows, but if you don't bother to write anything ON the stakes, this doesn't always help much.) (Besides, one year the dog pulled out all the stakes.)

"The Year of the Sunflower Genocide, SOMEBODY planted a row of them along the back of the garden, but kept this fact selfishly to himself.

"By summer, when the things were coming up, so were lots and lots of other large,

shabby, hairy-looking things — weeding being less popular around here than planting — all of which I was yanking up and throwing on the compost pile. I thought, while yanking, that it was peculiar that this one enormous breed of weed was growing in a row, but I put it down to a mathematical quirk of nature. By the time the sunflower planter pointed out (in loud, accusatory tones) my mistake, I had eliminated all sunflowers but one, which, I might add, did very well and got lots of attention, which is often the case with only children.

"That was also the year that Ethan, at age four, got his paws on all the tomato seedlings and planted them all by himself, squashing them upside down into little holes and burying them completely. However, this was not exactly a disaster, since they all did pretty well, and I will be ashamed until my dying day that I yelled at Ethan about it.

"Ethan says he can't remember this. He's a tactful child."

— *Rebecca Rupp, author of two wonderful plant histories:* **Blue Corn and Square Tomatoes** *and* **Red Oaks and Black Birches**

believe me? I'll prove it. Just dig there (*next* to where you planted, natch) with your trowel. See how the dirt just under the surface is still as bone dry as it was before you watered?

Nope, it takes a lot of watering to water well. So move your hose around enough to keep little runoff floods from washing your water somewhere else. Then keep coming back to the same areas until a trowel test shows you've penetrated underground as well as watered the surface.

Did I say you also have to water the sown area again and again and again anytime the soil begins to dry out? Yes, I did, but I'd better re-peat it — again and again and again — because I don't want you to forget.

When Things Don't Work

Suppose (just suppose) you do everything ol' Pat here has told you to do, and yet after days, then more days, then weeks, your constantly moistened seed *still* doesn't come up. How can this be? What went wrong?

The heck if I know! Maybe your timing was off — you planted too early in the year and they just rotted in the ground, or too late and it got too hot for that particular seed to want to sprout (see the Timing Chart on this page). Maybe your seed's too old (most seed can last for years if stored dry and not too hot, but some types — lettuce, for instance — get old quick). Maybe birds dug it all up

Timing: It's Not Everything, but It's a Lot!

A key factor in seed-starting success is when you plant. Some plants are early starters that love to get growing in those chilly days of early spring. (Indeed, in many climates, you can sow next year's rows of some of these — like spinach, lettuce, kale, calendulas, cosmos, pansies, dianthus, and snapdragon — in the fall for harvest or bloom the next spring!) Others, the late risers, will just sit in the soil (and maybe rot while they're waiting) until the ground has warmed up enough to suit their liking.

APPROXIMATE DATES FOR SOWING SEED OUTDOORS

As Early As Possible in Spring	Two to Four Weeks Before Last Frost	After Last Frost
Peas	Carrots	Beans
Beets	Onions	Corn
Kale	Potatoes	Cucumbers
Lettuce	Swiss Chard	Okra
Mustard Greens	Turnips	Pumpkins
Radishes	Calendulas	Winter Squash
Spinach	Marigolds	Zucchini
Alyssum	Nasturtiums	Cleome
Baby's Breath		Cosmos
Cornflower		Morning Glories
Larkspur		Portulaca
Stock		Sunflowers
		Zinnias

and ate it (crows are fond of newly sprouted corn seedlings, for example). Maybe you were sold a bunch of seed that's just no danged good (my favorite excuse).

Whatever the cause, it happens — at least, it sure does to *me*. You can replant (one reason to consider not planting all your seeds of one kind at once). Also, do some research. Some seeds have peculiar sprouting likes and dislikes. Spinach, for instance, germinates better if it's presoaked in warm water for eight hours or so before planting. (This works — honest.) Morning glories like it rough: they sprout better if you nick their hard seed coats with a file or knife.

Treat your failure as a mystery to be solved, a lesson to be learned. Ask other local gardeners what could be the matter. It's likely that some crop or flower becomes your particular nemesis (with me, it was peas) and takes you

Bare Beans

"I can laugh pretty hard at other gardeners' mistakes, because I've made some doozies of my own! Why, I remember about 30 years ago, pulling up my very first crop of bean seedlings when the seed pods sprouted and came out of the ground. I carefully stuck them all back in the ground the other way up. You see, I thought I had planted the seeds wrong side up!"

— *Warren Schroeder of Bowie, Maryland (Warren sent me this story after he read a tale in my magazine, GreenPrints, about a businessman-turned-gardener who pruned all the flowers from his tomato vines to get rid of "unwanted growth" . . . and then wondered why he didn't get any fruit!)*

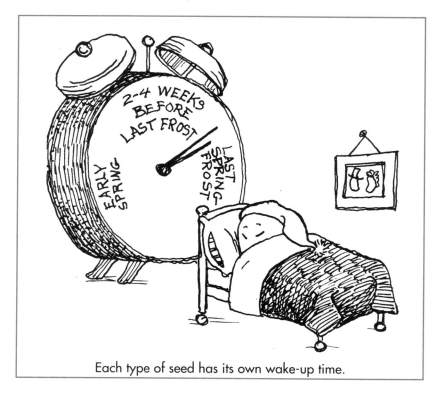

Each type of seed has its own wake-up time.

years to learn how to grow. Be disappointed, but not disheartened. It's all part of the Great Game of Gardening.

You can't fool a seed's nature, so pay attention to the planting times recommended in the chart. A key factor is the last frost date; that is, the average date of the last expected spring frost in your area. Your county extension agent will know that; so will experienced neighbor gardeners. Remember, though, it will vary depending on your own garden site. For instance, since cold air settles in valleys, I (a bottom dweller) get spring frosts later than my neighbors a half mile up the hill.

Of course, "average" last spring frost isn't necessarily the same as *this year's* last spring frost. Any garden planting timetable is an approximation, which you can fine-tune for your own site and locale as you gain experience. (In other words, don't sue *me* if you put those melon seeds in the week before a surprise late frost!)

7. TRANSPLANTING: THE TENDER ACT

GARDENER FINDS
Peace with Plants

As anyone who's ever crossed the threshold of a garden center in spring knows, seed sowing is only one way to get plants going in your garden. Indeed, all the plastic six-packs of 6-inch seedlings in those stores are meant to get you intoxicated with the *other* garden-starting technique — transplanting.

Works on me. Comes a Saturday in May when the weather's warm and the sun is high, I feel like going out to buy . . . a garden. I want to rush out and buy trays and trays of vegetable and flower starts (you know, all those plants I *should* have started from seed months ago). So I promise my waiting soil, "I'll be right back!" and drive down to the nearest garden center to stock up on starts.

There they are, shelves and shelves of plants that, like pups in a pet store, are just begging me to take them home. The pansies call out first. "See our bright faces! Wouldn't we look cheery clumped around your mailbox or lined along the walk?"

Yes, they would, and only $1.50 a six-pack? I'll need a pickup to hold the pansies I purchase!

Next, my wandering eye spots some trays of tomatoes. Look at those foot-high wonders! As hot as it is today, surely it's time to set out tomatoes!

But I can't leave them sitting out in the vegetable patch all alone. I'll have to get some little lettuces, infant eggplants, bantam broccolis, and prepubescent peppers to go with them. And, me oh my, I didn't even *know* you could buy leek plants!

Ah, here are some herbs: thyme, sage, rosemary, oregano. My garden will smell like something's already cooking!

And over there — Good morning, geraniums! Ummm, good month for marigolds. Oooo, let's snap up some snapdragons. Who me, impatiens? Why, certainly. . . .

My eyes were bigger than my garden!

You get the point: the first mistake of transplanting is buying too many transplants! Still, succumbing to the one-more-sixpack impulse is a common, but not major, offense. So Stone's not going to chide you too hard if you commit this one. (Aren't I nice?)

47

Besides, transplanting is one of my own favorite garden activities. Taking those sheltered, infant seedlings and moving them out into the cold, real world of the garden is one of the most tender of horticultural acts. No act in gardening reminds me more of parenting than transplanting. (Hmm. Maybe that's why plant-raising businesses are called *nurseries*.)

Before I get into specific do's and don'ts, let me point out that the process is identical whether you're putting out purchased or home-grown starts. I'm assuming here that you're putting out purchased seedlings only because I haven't covered indoor seed starting yet. It's a somewhat sophisticated gardening skill, so I'm saving it for later in the book. In real life I prefer to put out young plants I've reared myself.

All right, it's time to move from the nursery — to the garden!

There are two transplanting goofs that gardeners make so often I'd better cover them right up front.

Transplanting Faux Pas #1: Setting plants out too early.

For a gardener, spring fever is that urge to get those plants out there so they can grow, grow, grow! Every year, when that deceptive "Indian-spring" warm spell hits, far too many of us start putting out frost-tender tomatoes and geraniums.

Don't. Don't believe your senses on those too-early warm days. Instead, time your transplanting by the date of the average last spring frost in your area. (Broccoli, for instance, can be set out a month before that date. Tomatoes, though, should stay indoors until that date or a week or so later.)

Transplanting Faux Pas #2: Setting plants out without first acclimating them to the outdoors.

Beware the Friend Bearing Plants

"Sometimes people give you plants because they have too many of them. And why do they have too many of them? It may well be because they're the kind of rambunctious rambler that once they start growing, they never stop.

"I used to work at a botanical garden. One day a volunteer came in and gave me a sickly little pot of Silver King artemesia. The director came by, took one look, and said, 'That thing'll never live.' I took the poor thing home to try to resuscitate it. And it lived, all right, it lived. It spread all over the garden. It was three years before I got it all pulled out.

"I used to grow gooseneck loosestrife. It's a white-flowered plant that turns a nice shade of red in fall. But it also sends out cast-iron roots yards away from its base. It took me several years to get all those roots out. Then I made the mistake of throwing them on the compost pile.

"That fall, my husband — who does *not* do the weeding and consequently liked the loosestrife a lot more than I did — suddenly said, "Oh, look! There's that flower I've been missing so much!" Yep, it had spread all through my compost pile! It's a good thing I hadn't yet put any of that compost on my garden!"

— *Susan McClure, author of*
The Herb Gardener, who lives and
gardens near Chicago, Illinois

Hardening off, the first of the seven steps of transplanting, is crucial. Seedlings lead a pampered life, whether they were raised on your windowsill or in a commercial greenhouse. They have enjoyed ideal growing conditions: constant warmth, lots of light, and plenty to eat and drink. Now they're about to be thrown out into a world of drying winds, chilling nights, and harsh sun. (Harsh sun? Yes, too much direct sun can actually burn tender seedlings until they've had time to form cartenoids, pigments that act as sort of a short-term sunscreen.)

The Eternal Virgin

"I'm the eternal virgin. Every winter I make the same silly but heartrending mistake of overordering new plants. You should keep every nursery bill and used order form in front of you before you ever send off for something new. Otherwise, like me, you'll end up with endless boxes of plants, running around, going, 'Where can I tuck this? Where can I tuck that?'

"I'll tell you something: it takes *time* to really make mistakes. If you don't have much time for gardening, you're fairly careful about what you do. Then when you're tempted to try some new plants or projects, you listen to that quiet voice inside your head that says, 'Don't.' But if you figure you can spare a little extra effort, you ignore that little voice. The end result is devastation — every time."
— *Peter Loewer, of Asheville, North Carolina, the author of more than twenty gardening books including* The Evening Garden *and* Seeds: The Definitive Guide to Growing, History, and Lore

You don't send your children out into the world without first doing all you can to prepare them for what's ahead. Do the same with your plants. Harden them off by giving them some practice at handling cool weather and stem-stiffening breezes. And don't forget that, at least at first, you need to bring them in at night. It's no fun stepping outside in the morning and discovering that a whole tray of carefully nurtured seedlings has frozen stiff. (I know.)

After you've hardened off your seedlings, set them out with all the tenderness prescribed in the sequence shown below. Shortcutting these steps may not kill your plants (then again, it may), but it will certainly slow their growth. It can even shock them into thinking they're going to die, so they rush to bloom or produce fruit before they're big enough to give you the show or bounty you'd hoped for.

So remember: TLC — Transplants Love Care. OK, here we go with . . .

The Seven Steps of Transplanting

1. Harden Them Off

To help your seedlings toughen up for their new life in the outdoors, **set them outside for a few hours every day.** Make the transition gradual. At first set them out only on sunny, calm days. Bit by bit, build up their hardiness by putting them outdoors for longer periods, during cooler days, and through warmer nights. After a week or two they should be able to tough it out outdoors full time.

2. Pick the Right Time

Obviously, you shouldn't transplant a tender annual when a cold front is one day away. Just as important, pick the right time of day for the

Water transplants well.

big moving-out operation. **Set the young plants out in the late afternoon, early evening, or — best yet — during a spell of cloudy weather.** Why? Because transplanting is a shock to a plant's system. Until its roots have settled in and gotten well established in their new home, hot, dry weather can suck moisture out of the leaves faster than the roots can replace it.

3. Water the Roots

Want to know a quick way to kill a plant? Let its roots dry out (works every time). Since you don't want that to happen, **water seedlings well** before you pull them out of their trays or flats. Keep them wrapped in a damp cloth if they'll be sitting out in the air before being dug in.

4. Dig

Make the hole **wide enough** to handle the full set of spread-out roots. And make it **deep enough** so the plant's base will sit at the same depth at which it has been growing.

5. Set the Plant in the Hole

Important: **Handle the plant by the root-ball (best choice) or leaves (second best), but**

Putting Labels — and Plants — in the Wrong Place

"Oh, everyone forgets to label ornamental plants, so then they can't tell what they are or accidentally dig up the roots in the off-season because they don't remember they're there. And we've all used non-permanent labels that deteriorate and become as useless as no labels at all.

"No, my labeling mistake is more sophisticated than that. I'm not always consistent about *where* I put my plant labels. Why does that matter? Because how can you tell if the roots of a plant are in front of or behind a label unless you have a habit of always putting your labels in the same spot relative to your plants?"
— *Marty Ross of Kansas City, Missouri, a syndicated garden columnist for Universal Press as well as a regular garden columnist for the Kansas City Star*

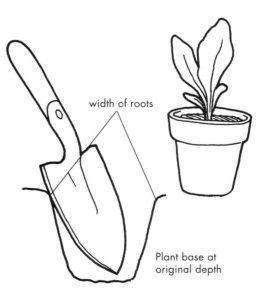

width of roots

Plant base at original depth

Four Steps for Buying Good Transplants

Not all store bought seedlings are the same — in fact, some are definitely worth *avoiding*. Here are a few smart-shopper tips for transplanters:

1. Buy plants "green."

Don't buy starts in fruit or flower. Such precocious youngsters may look appealing, but most of them are really old before their time, prematurely reaching the end of their life cycle instead of just beginning it.

2. Steer clear of too-large plants.

Again, they look great, but if they're too big for their pots, root growth has been restricted. (If you shake such a plant out of its pot, you may find roots that have circled around in their container like a caged animal.) Small, healthy plants can grow into big ones surprisingly quickly. Plants with restricted, damaged roots may never recover.

3. Look out for disease.

If you see *any* sign of rot, such as soft, black lesions at the base of the stem, splotches on the leaves, or bumps on the roots, *don't* buy that plant. You'll have enough plant disease in your garden, believe me, without importing extra pathogen problems.

4. Watch out for extreme legginess or yellowing.

Since commercial seedlings frequently get crowded in their trays, they're often a bit long stemmed or have a couple of yellowing lower leaves. That's all right; they should recover once give some room to stretch in your garden. But if they're overly miscolored or so scrawny they can't even stand up, forget 'em.

---

not by that apparently obvious handle, the stem. Leave it alone. The stem is the lifeline of the plant. And there's only one. Injure it — you'll kill the plant.

Even if you have trouble getting the plant out of its pot, don't pull on the stem. Turn the pot upside down and (holding the soil ball) tap hard on the bottom of the container. You can gently poke a stick through the drainage hole(s) to push the rootball out.

For roots that were tightly packed in their container ("root bound"), tease them out a bit by hand to encourage them to spread. Likewise, if the plant grew in a peat pot, lightly tear that pot to help those roots start roving.

6. Water It Well

Plant roots need oxygen, but they absorb it from the soil, not directly from the air. Air pockets left in the ground can injure or kill exposed roots. So tamp the dirt firmly around the plant with your hands and then water it thoroughly. Water will promote good root-to-soil contact as well as help reduce the shock to the plant.

7. Shelter the Plant from Extreme Weather

Assuming you guessed right and the weather stays mild, you shouldn't need to protect your transplant. But if the weather suddenly makes a serious extreme turn, you may need to come to a seedling's temporary defense. Cover tender plants when an unexpected frost is due. Upside-down trash buckets or cardboard boxes, old blankets supported by sticks (try to keep the cover from touching the plant), or a thick mulch of loose hay may do the job. If a spell of blazing sun hits right after you transplant, try to give the starts some form of temporary shading.

■ ■ ■ ■ ■

That's pretty much it for the mechanics. The actual process — ah, that goes much deeper. There's something so soothing, so bonding about nestling seedlings in the soil that it may feel like *you* are setting roots in the garden — as well as your plants.

ALL THE DIRT on SOIL

I wasn't loyal to my soil — and [country-western guitar chords here] — it wasn't loyal to me.

Once upon a time (way back in Chapter 5), I promised you that we'd be making a future visit to the biology classroom, where we'd learn one of the keys to ongoing gardening success: soil building.

Well, guess what? Here we are! It's time to step back for a little while from the weeks of digging and tilling and sowing and planting to date *and* the months of weeding and watering and picking and replanting to come . . . and take some time to ponder the basics of growing *soil* as well as crops and flowers.

Back in ol' Chapter 5, I told you how to supply enough fertility to your soil to overcome any initial glaring deficiencies and get your plants off to a good start. But that's like getting a free tank of gas when you buy a new car — in the long run, it won't get you very far. To keep your garden thriving for weeks, seasons, and years, you need to provide it with an ongoing improvement program.

A Rose is a Rose is a . . . Dahlia?

"I was touring a large, large wholesale nursery with its owner. He thought I knew everything about botany and horticulture — after all, I was the Garden Editor for the *Sacramento Bee*. The truth was I knew nothing. I had recently come over from the Sports Department and was learning on the fly. So, as we walked along, I was just trying to keep my mouth shut . . . until we came to a big greenhouse and I couldn't help but say, 'Oh, look! Roses!'

"The owner was so stunned he just stared at me. Then he muttered, 'Some people think they look like roses, but they really are dahlias.' He was as embarrassed for me as I was for myself!

"That shook me up. I started taking night classes in horticulture and really got serious about the subject. Now I know the difference between dahlias and roses: dahlias don't fight back!"
— *Dick Tracy, garden editor for the* Sacramento Bee

This will do two things: keep your soil's fertility up and improve its texture. The need for the former is obvious: plants use up soil nutrients. They need a continual replenishment of Misters N, P, and K and all their minor mineral cousins — especially N, that oh-so-basic element that's also oh-so-ephemeral many soil tests don't even try to measure it.

The need for the latter? Soil with good texture — with lots of crumbly, friable humus — has so many virtues it's hard to list them all. It both retains *and* drains water; that is, unlike sandy soil that lets water rush right through or clay soil that gets waterlogged, it holds the "just right" amount of water for plants under the widest range of conditions. Well-textured ground retains soil nutrients, releasing them gradually over time (like a time-release capsule) as its components slowly break down. It

holds air (a full 25 percent of healthy soil is air) for plant roots.

Healthy soil also encourages the growth of soil microorganisms. According to one estimate, a single teaspoonful of fertile soil contains 4 billion bacteria, 40 to 100 meters of mold filament (mold filament — gotta love it), 144,000,000 actinomycetes (half-fungi, half-bacteria creatures), and large quantities of algae and other microoganisms. All of these, along with the organic matter that sustains them, transform inert, mineral dirt into healthy, living soil.

Soil with good texture also encourages earthworms. A whole book could be written about the virtues of earthworms (indeed, Charles Darwin spent *two decades* of his life studying the subterranean earth builders and wrote one). Since doing so here, however, would make

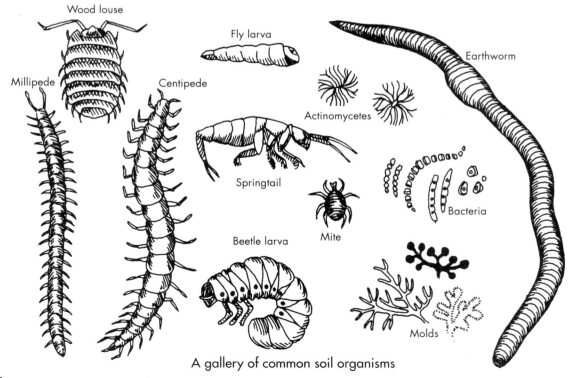

A gallery of common soil organisms

Chapter 8 a tad lengthy, suffice it to say that earthworms — up to a half million per acre in healthy soil — aerate up to 5 tons of soil per acre per year, and make nutrients much, much more available by ingesting soil and excreting droppings — uh, "castings" — that are five times as rich in available nitrogen, phosphorus, and potassium as the surrounding soil.

Pick up a double handful of healthy soil and you'll be holding more microorganisms than there are people on earth — a veritable biological super factory of fertility (ta dah!). How do you create such an industrial park of pulsatingly powerful soil productivity in your own yard? Three words: add organic matter.

Which is to say, feed your soil, not your plants! And there, of course, you have the **First Big Mistake of Chapter 8** (you *were* waiting for this, weren't you?): failing to care for your soil first and continually. You don't want to feed your soil once, then forget it. You want to engage in a regular soil building (like body building) program.

Unfortunately, putting this particular activity in the imperative makes it sound so burdensome — like regular dental check ups or something. Truth is, though, growing soil, like growing plants, is kind of fun. Indeed, many are the gardeners who, with a proud gleam in their eye, love to show a visitor their *soil* as well as their plants.

And well they should because let's not ignore the fact that while soil building is fun, it's *work* fun. A good exercise regimen is fun, too, but you work up a sweat doing it. Same here.

OK, one last comment before we head outside and start pumping compost. Soil building does **not** mean throwing handfuls of chemical fertilizer on your garden every few weeks. Chemical fertilizers, with their sudden flushes of nutrients, do nothing to improve soil texture and can actually harm microorganisms. Since they readily wash out of the soil (not being fixed by those wonderful aggregates of humus) they create feast-or-famine nutrient conditions. True, you can grow food — and flowers — entirely on a chemical fertilizer diet (Hello, American agriculture!), but they will not withstand pests or stress as well as soil-nourished plants, nor will they be as nutritious.

Soil-Building Strategies

In certain religions, one step on the path to enlightenment is to sit in the lotus position and chant "OMMMMM." That, in two letters, is the game here: O.M. Organic Matter — both the medium and the fuel of soil fertility. It provides the place for all those wonderful soil creatures to live and the stuff they'll consume as they improve and fertilize your soil.

The one new variation to the chant is that you want to learn to say "OM" in as many different ways as possible. In other words, the more ways you can incorporate organic matter into your soil, the better!

O.M. #1: Mulch

We've already covered one way to add organic matter to your soil: mulch. Mulch, along with its weed-smothering, water-retaining, and soil-cooling virtues, provides an ongoing supply of O.M. to the soil beneath it as it breaks down. It's a very successful way to build up soil (Mother Nature uses it all the time), but, well, it is kind of slow (Mother Nature's never been one to rush). In addition, *fresh* mulch (such as fresh sawdust) consumes nitrogen in its first breakdown stages, so a green mulch can temporarily absorb that nutrient.

All in all, though, adding mulch is definitely

Mulch is a slow but sure way to build soil.

a fine way to improve the organic matter content of your soil. After all, there are those deep-mulch gardeners (the late Ruth Stout was their patron saint) who maintain perfectly good gardens by doing nothing more than continually piling on more and more mulch!

O.M. #2: Crop Rotation

I'm cheating here: crop rotation is *not* a way to add organic matter to your garden. The real reason I'm sneaking crop rotation in here is that it does help *balance* the fertility in your garden, as well as reduce plant disease and pest problems . . . and both these things are important for a healthy garden.

(An aside: crop rotation, as the name implies, is generally a technique associated with vegetable gardens. At least, I haven't heard anyone talk about *flower* rotation! Still, if a flower I was raising in one spot seemed, each year, to get more disease or bug problems, I'd certainly grow it somewhere else.)

If you let them, crop rotation patterns can get pretty complicated. Let's keep it simple. First, look at nutrition. Leaf crops generally need a lot of nitrogen (N), fruit crops generally need a lot of phosphorous (P), and root crops generally have a fairly high potassium (K) requirement. (Cole crops — like broccoli, cabbage, cauliflower, and Brussels sprouts — are treated as leaf crops in this analysis, like their leafy cousins, kale and collards.) Try not to plant leaf, fruit, or root crops twice in a row in the same place, but spread them around so that the same spot in the garden grows a leaf, fruit, or root no more than once every three growing periods.

Second, let's look at disease and pest prevention. Many diseases are soil borne, and many insect pests overwinter in the soil. So if you move a crop they like to a different area of the garden, it'll be harder for the bugs (both kinds) to get to that crop next year.

The trick here is to think of vegetable families, not just individual crops. The same pests that bother melons pester their kin, cucumbers. The critters that nibble cabbage also enjoy a meal of cauliflower. So try to rotate the following *family groups* in your garden:

Cucurbitaceae (cucumber): cucumbers, melons, pumpkins, squash

Cruciferae (mustard): broccoli, Brussels sprouts, cabbage, cauliflower, collards, kale, kohlrabi, mustard, radishes, turnips

Solanaceae (tomato): eggplants, peppers, potatoes, tomatoes

Umbelliferae (carrot): carrots, dill, parsley, parsnips

Liliaceae (onion): garlic, leeks, onions, scallions, shallots

Chenopodiaceae (beet): beets, Swiss chard, spinach

O.M. #3: Cover Cropping

Now we get to one of my favorite ways to say OM. Cover crops are a fascinating and fun way to add organic matter to your soil. They also have

Rotate your plantings by nutrient requirements.

side benefits, such as reducing erosion and even — O gardener's joy — beating out weeds!

Yet for some unknown reason, I'd say most gardeners don't grow cover crops! This is a big mistake. Yes, indeed, *not* cover cropping has to rank as (shudder!) the **Second Big Mistake of Chapter 8.**

What are cover crops? They are crops grown for the purpose of improving your soil. Sometimes called green manures, most cover crops are grown for a few weeks, then turned under into the soil before they bear seeds or get hard and woody. Used this way, they directly add a crop of organic matter to the soil. It's like composting in place, or *growing soil!*

Cover crops have other uses, as well. Leguminous covers, such as vetch or clover, have root nodules that fix nitrogen and so provide extra nitrogen for the next crop grown in that spot. (It's helpful to inoculate legume seeds with the appropriate rhizobia bacteria before

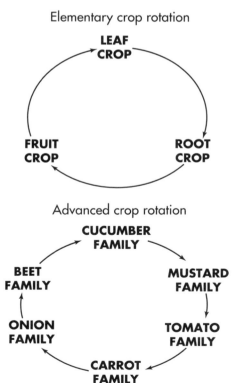

Elementary crop rotation

LEAF
CROP

FRUIT
CROP

ROOT
CROP

Advanced crop rotation

CUCUMBER
FAMILY

BEET
FAMILY

MUSTARD
FAMILY

ONION
FAMILY

TOMATO
FAMILY

CARROT
FAMILY

SOIL BUILDING

57

Soil Sorrows

"I don't believe in the garden mystique, that some people naturally have a green thumb. There are no green thumbs, I say, just sore backs. That, and experience gained the hard way.

"Myself, I've made gardening mistakes on soil both good and poor. The first year I gardened was in mid-Pennsylvania, Amish country. The soil was a wonderful, rich loam. I was so excited, I went right out after a rain and started digging my new garden. I dug and dug and dug. You know what happened: the soil hardened into brick-hard lumps. It took me the rest of the summer to beat them out with a hoe.

"One time I gardened down in the sand hills of South Carolina. The soil was nothing but sand. Still, I honestly thought that if I kept putting the compost and organic matter to it, I'd end up with decent soil. Never did — the sand swallowed it up. I realized later I should have used raised beds and created good soil on top of the sand instead of trying to improve it.

"Now I grow in North Carolina clay. I mulched it really heavily the first year and the soil quality really improved. I felt pretty smug about what I'd done, so didn't bother to mulch the second year. By the third, my garden had all reverted to clay that was hard as rock. I didn't realize you have to keep putting the organic matter to clay if you want it to get — and keep — good soil."

— *Sara Pitzer of Richfield, North Carolina, author of* Buying and Selling Antiques

you plant it to help its nitrogen-fixing capacity. Just ask the person who sold you the seed what powder to use and shake the seed in a bag with the powder before planting.)

Fast- and thick-growing cover crops like buckwheat or annual rye can beat out or "smother" weeds, actually *eliminating* a pesky, invasive weed. For instance, to rid a flower or vegetable bed of that pernicious garden nuisance, quackgrass, plant the area thickly in annual rye as soon as the soil can be worked in the spring. When the last frost date comes, mow down the rye, till in its roots, and plant a thick patch of heat-loving buckwheat. Once a month turn the buckwheat under, and plant more. Then in fall sow winter rye. By the next spring your plot should be cleansed of persistent weed troubles! (If this sounds like a lot of work, you haven't been gardening long enough to know what *real* work is . . . namely, infinitely pulling a perennially persistent weed!)

Cover crops can also be used to overwinter sections of your garden that otherwise would be open and exposed to erosion for months at a time. Winter rye, for instance, will start growing in the fall, and — in most areas — survive winter, then put on a new spurt of growth in the spring. Or (experiment!) you might grow annual rye in the fall. In your area it may winterkill and make a nice in-place mulch for next spring's planting. Or combine either rye with a hardy vetch — hairy vetch is most popular — which adds nitrogen to the soil and seems to have other benefits, as well. (A hot new idea among tomato growers these days is sticking their tomato plants in a chopped-down but not turned-under bed of overwintered hairy vetch. Yields have been outstanding.)

All of these uses are in addition to the old, main reason for growing cover crops: to add green matter to the soil.

So you can see why some gardeners are so excited about cover crops. Indeed, some C.C. advocates think you should have half of your garden in cover crops at all times — and just switch the area you use for your food or annual flowers and the cover-crop section back and forth. (I've started doing this myself — partly because I finally admitted to myself that my garden's been too danged big!) Others say a third of your garden at any time should be in cover crops. That's a good goal, too, and certainly to your garden's benefit.

Your goals don't have to be so grandiose. But, for certain, **(1) work cover crops into your crop rotation scheme.** That way, you'll be rotating not three elements, but four: root, leaf, fruit, *and* cover crops. Along with that, **(2) plant cover crops any other chance you get.** Start looking for the opportunities, and you'll find them.

Cover crops are a cinch to grow. Just work up the soil enough so you can plant (you don't need to make it super smooth). Broadcast the seed, sowing thickly by hand, first in one direction and then perpendicular to it. Then lightly rake over the area to cover the seed.

The most complicated thing with cover crops is choosing which ones to use! There're a scillion choices, including a leafy green with the unfortunate name of rape. No doubt, the queen of green manures is alfalfa. A deep-rooted nitrogen fixer, alfalfa is perhaps the most famous soil-building crop of all. But to get real benefit from it, you need to let it grow for at least a year (you can cut it back occasionally and compost the cuttings). I don't normally have a section of my garden that I'm willing to let grow as cover for over a year, so I haven't yet grown alfalfa . . . but I'd sure like to.

I can't begin to cover all the cover crops, so

I'll just mention the most popular ones, all of which I've used.

Buckwheat. This champion weed-smothering crop grows so fast you won't believe it and makes a little grassy field topped by lovely, small white flowers. Very easy to turn under. Only grows in warm weather. Not a nitrogen fixer, but great for adding green matter.

Clover. Clovers are as easy to turn under as buckwheat and have the added advantage of adding N to the soil. White or red are popular varieties, and seeds are readily available.

Hairy vetch. A graceful, delicate legume with purple flowers, hairy vetch is quite cold hardy. It can be a little hard to get a thick stand of it, so it's often grown with a rye (especially winter rye) to provide more soil cover and give the vetch support.

Rye. Annual for spring, winter for overwintering. A great volume of tall, grassy growth. Winter rye can be mowed as needed the following spring to keep it under control until you're ready to turn it under.

Soybean. Another nitrogen fixer, one that provides a good leafy soil cover. Turn it under before it flowers or most of the N value will go into the seeds.

The real work involved with cover crops (well there had to be *some*) comes after they've grown. How do you turn them under? It can be pretty hard to do by hand. If possible, I like to mow my cover crop down — it chops the plants into small pieces that turn under easily and decompose rapidly. Then I till the cuttings and roots under with my rototiller. If the crop's too big to mow, you can cut it with a weed eater, swing blade, or (my preference) scythe. Then rake the cuttings off to compost (thus add to the soil later), and turn under the roots.

I'd feel a little guilty if I didn't warn you of one thing: winter rye roots can be pretty danged hard to turn under. The longer the plants grow, the clumpier the roots get. So, while I used to mow and let grow my winter rye for as long as possible in spring, I now turn it under as soon — and as young — as I can.

Also, don't plant vegetables or flowers in a cover-cropped area until at least three weeks after you turn the cover crop under. It takes that long for the green matter to begin to break down.

Undercropping. I can't let this topic go without covering one more, truly cool way of cover cropping: *undercropping*. New England garden expert Eliot Coleman has perfected this idea. Basically, you let the main crop in an area get a head start in growth, then all around it (where the weeds like to grow) plant a low-growing cover crop to add nutrition to the soil while beating back weeds.

The key is: **plant your undercrop precisely four to five weeks after your main crop.** (Indeed, one hidden advantage to this technique is it motivates you to keep after small weeds early on so the undersowing area will be weed free when you plant it.) For short crops, dwarf white clover is probably the best undersown companion. For taller ones, sweet clover, vetch, red clover, alsike clover, or even soybeans will do.

Undercropping is a great way to have your crop and fertilize your next one, too! Give it a try!

■ ■ ■ ■ ■

O.M. #4: Famous and Fabulous, It's . . .

Well, now, you may think I spent quite a bit of time on my third method of getting organic matter into your garden, cover cropping — and I have. Cover cropping is terrific!

But you ain't seen nothin' yet. Indeed, my fourth and final O.M. boosting technique is so important that I'm going to devote a whole chapter to it. We're talking, of course, about that amazing, dynamic, renowned, fantastic soil-building technique known as . . .

BLACK GOLD
Found in Garden!

You knew I was going to say composting, didn't you? Heck, people who wouldn't know which end of a hoe to hold have heard about compost. In fact, even if you've never touched a handful of that legendary soil builder in your life, you probably already have some well-formed opinions about compost.

Common Prejudices Against Compost

- **It's overhyped.** Compost is talked about like some miracle cure. Nothing's that good.
- **It's hippie stuff.** Only organic fanatics use it.

It is garden gold or hippie hooey?

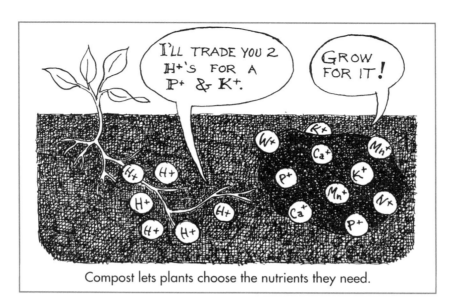

Compost lets plants choose the nutrients they need.

- **It smells bad.**
- **It looks gross.** Gardens are supposed to be beautiful. Who wants a big pile of dead, rotting, varmint-attracting garbage sitting in their yard?
- **It takes too much work.**

Well, gardening brothers and sisters, if you hold any of these opinions about composting, you are — guess what? — mistaken! Yes, that is the **Big Goof of Chapter 9:** having a preconceived *negative* notion about compost. So before we get into the mechanics of this chapter's subject, let me first go through the negative opinions about it:

1. It's overhyped. "Black gold" . . . "Plant manna" . . . "The elixir of the garden." Compost does get a whole pile of good press, but — take note — this praise doesn't come mainly from salesmen or advertisements, but from *gardeners!* Experienced gardeners. Flower and food. Chemical and organic.

Why? Because compost does everything a good source of organic matter should do. It both retains and drains water. It releases nutrients slowly. It encourages soil microorganisms and earthworms.

And compost — hold on to your trowels — does even more. It moderates pH, helping to bring the soil's acid-alkaline balance into that pH 6.5–7.0 range most garden plants prefer. It helps plants resist pests and disease. (Indeed, it even *deters* several soil diseases.) It adds trace minerals and helps fix toxins like heavy metals in the soil. Ladies and gentlemen, it even helps plants produce their own growth stimulators.

Let's look more closely at just one of compost's virtues, nutrient retention. Most soil nutrients in compost exist as positively charged molecules, called *cations*. The negatively charged molecules in compost attract and hold these nutrient cations. Plant roots, surrounded by their auras of positive hydrogen ions, then come along and make friendly exchanges, giving up some of their hydrogen ions for the nutrient ions of their choice. Plants thus *choose* for themselves the nutrients in compost they need!

Since most of those nutrients are not "free,"

they don't show up well on soil tests. Compost thus generally gets low N-P-K scores. But plants don't read soil tests. They know what's really growing on.

And, since most of those nutrients are not "free," they don't wash out easily. In lab tests, some well-composted soil got washed with the equivalent of a dozen drenching summer rainstorms — seven times its own weight in water — without losing an appreciable amount of nutrients!

In sum, although compost certainly *is* hyped (I admit I sometimes get tired of hearing about it myself), it's not *over*hyped. Its kudos are well earned.

2. It's that hippie stuff just for the organic fanatics. If you really think that, you haven't met many gardeners. Go to any garden club meeting, from "Little Ladies of the African Violet" to "Classy Connoisseurs of Conifers," and you'll find plenty of compost advocates there. Gardeners who use a lot of chemical fertilizers and those who use none both know compost is a major "good guy" for their soils.

3. Compost smells bad. Nope, finished compost, from a distance, has no smell at all. Up close — in the hand — it smells rich and earthy. A composting compost pile will normally have no particular smell, either. If it does give off a rotten or ammonia-like odor, you're doing something wrong. Later on in this chapter, I'll show you what that is — and how to correct it.

4. It's gross. A big pile of composting plant material — to a true gardener — is a sight to cherish and sigh (enviously) over. To the uninitiated, well, I suppose it *could* look like just a big pile of dead plants. If you find a compost pile unattractive (or are afraid your neighbors will), then locate your pile out of sight behind some shrubs, enclose it in a homemade bin or commercial composter, or try the buried-in-place trench composting technique I will cover later.

5. It takes too much work. Whoops! This criticism *does* have merit (oh, well, four out of five ain't bad): composting *is* work. But how much work it involves depends entirely on you, and how quickly you want to get the finished product. Basically, the quicker you want the compost, the harder you'll have to work for it. If you want your black gold in a few weeks, you're going to have to shred all the pile's ingredients (a good bit of work) and turn the pile every few days (ditto). If you're willing, like me, to wait a year for your reward, you can completely forget both those steps. You will then have only the one-time labor of gathering the materials and building the pile.

If that still seems like too much work, you can take an easier, to-be-described way out: trench composting. If even *that* seems burdensome to you, well, hey, there're plenty of places to *buy* compost these days.

Let's Start Cooking

You can make compost one of two ways: cool or hot. Cool compost basically sits there and slowly decomposes — OK, rots — over time. Hot compost literally heats up, to a sizzling 140° or 160°F. The latter process has some advantages: it's a lot faster. Heat kills many weed seeds and diseases that may have been in the original plant material. And it's fun. Seeing the steam rise off your brewing compost pile on a cool autumn morn is a warm moment of gardener's joy. (You'll know you really have compost fever when you plunge your arm into the pile to find out if it's too hot to stand!)

But cool composting works, too. It makes perfectly good compost (some say better, on the idea that less nutrient energy is burned off as heat). It just takes longer.

Either way, you'll probably get the hang of composting quicker if you think of it as a green fire. A campfire needs four things to burn: fuel, heat, spark, and air. A compost pile needs its four equivalents:

Brown Matter = Fuel
Green Matter = Heat
Soil = Spark
Air = Air

Brown matter. That's dead plant material: dried leaves, hay, straw, partly dried garden debris, shredded stalks. These things are loaded with *carbon*. This is, by bulk, the main ingredient of your compost fire.

Green matter. This is fresh plant material. It's a good source of *nitrogen* — the main source of heat in composting. Fresh green plants (especially those nitrogen-fixing legumes) and kitchen wastes are two sources. Fresh animal manure is another great nitrogen source. If you're low on either, you can buy N-rich amendments like blood meal, bone meal, cottonseed meal, hoof and horn meal, or alfalfa meal.

Soil. Your pile will work more quickly if you add beneficial *microorganisms* — the guys that actually do the composting — to it as you go. The easiest way is to work in healthy garden soil; it already contains such good guys. Or you can buy a commercial compost-pile activator (available from most garden supply companies) to give your pile its initial bacterial "spark."

Air. Plant material can decompose in one of two ways: aerobically (with air) or anaerobi-

A sight to warm a gardener's heart

cally (without air). The former is quick and smells fine; the latter is slow and stinks (it's called rotting). To get the former, you'll need to make sure your pile can "breathe," that air can get into the heart of it.

That covers the basic concept. Let's get cooking.

Building a Compost Pile

I'm not going to spend much time on cool composting. All you do with that is pile up your ingredients, cover them with a tarp or straw so nutrients won't leach out, and leave them alone for a year or two or three.

The skill — and thrill — of composting comes in making hot compost. Why do I say "skill"? Because there's a technique involved here, namely getting the right proportions of carbon-rich (brown) and nitrogen-rich (green) ingredients. Compost theoreticians say that the official ratio of carbon to nitrogen should be about 25 to 1, an intimidating-sounding and utterly useless statement to most gardeners. (Nobody I know keeps track of the C-to-N ratio of the various ingredients in their compost piles, believe me.)

In real life, the point is you need more carbon-rich material than nitrogen-rich material, and sometimes it may take a bit of fiddling to get the proportions right, depending on what materials you have on hand to compost. Shepherd Ogden, owner of The Cook's Garden seed company, feels a good rule-of-thumb is using four to five times as much carbon-rich material as nitrogen-rich material. My neighbor (and former head gardener for *The Mother Earth News* magazine), Susan Sides, likes a 5:5:2 pattern: a 5-inch layer of green matter, a 5-inch layer of brown matter, and a 2-inch layer of animal manure. Eliot Coleman, Maine grower

and author, alternates a 3-inch layer of dry, brown material with a 1- to 6-inch layer of green matter (1-inch with dense green matter like kitchen scraps or grass clippings, 6-inch with loose, open material like tomato stems or bean vines).

All these formulas work. In any case, *layer* your ingredients. Start on bare, loosened earth — so earthworms and microorganisms in the soil can have a chance to move up into your pile. Then, to help aerate the pile, either put down a layer of sticks or (my preference) the fluffiest brown matter you have. Add a layer of green matter. Then put on a thin layer of soil, manure, or commercial compost activator to "spark" your biological fire.

From then on alternate brown, green, and spark layers. Your pile needs to be at least 3 to 4 feet on a side and just as tall to have enough internal mass to heat up well. And if your materials are dry, dampen them some with a hose as you go. The ingredients need to be damp, not soggy, to compost. As the old gardener's expression (originated by the father of modern

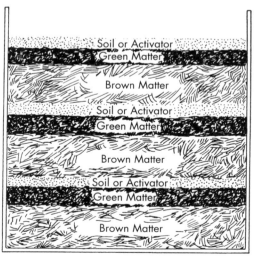

Layer your compost pile.

day composting, Sir Albert Howard) goes, the pile should be "damp as a wrung-out sponge." Once you're finished, cover the top with a tarp or thick layer of straw to help hold heat in and keep rain out (too much rain might leach out nutrients or make the pile too soggy).

If you build a bin for your compost, try to make at least one side removable (ideally, board by board) to make it easier to fill. Actually, the ideal bin has two compartments: one to build the initial pile, another for turn-ing that pile into. Well, *actually* actually, the ideal bin has *three* compartments: the third holds a finished (or almost finished) pile of compost while the other two are used for the next one you're making.

If all goes well, in a few days the interior of your pile should start to heat up (you can poke a plastic-covered meat thermometer or your arm in there to see). Gradually, the inside of the pile should get downright hot. If so, congratulations! You're composting in style!

After a couple of weeks the pile will begin to cool down. To get the quickest results, *that* is when you should turn the pile, mixing the parts that were on the outside into the inside. The new mixing and air supply should start another heating cycle. Many people will let it age on its own after that. Others will turn the pile one more time.

The end result should be a dark, fertile mound of gardener's gold. If the compost is complete, you won't be able to identify any of the original ingredients. You can still use it if it's only partly done, but the less finished the compost, the longer you should wait until planting in a spot.

Embalmed by Mulch

"My number one garden mistake is to mulch with uncomposted material. I remember the summer I mulched my vegetable garden with old newspapers and loads and loads of fresh bark. Maybe it was the acidity of the bark or the way it drains nitrogen from the soil, but my eggplants, tomatoes, and peppers acted like they were frozen in time. They reminded me of ants petrified in amber. They didn't die. They just did nothing — for a very long time.

"You would think I'd have learned my lesson from that, but the vision of having a picture-perfect, weed-free garden (without spending every living moment tending to it) still gains the upper hand. Why, did you know you can even turn a *zucchini plant* into a puny thing by tucking nice fresh bark mulch up to its chinny chin chin? You can, I'm here to testify. I pulled off this feat only last year!"

— Elizabeth Hunter, who lives in
Bakersville, North Carolina,
writes a regular column
for Blue Ridge Country magazine.

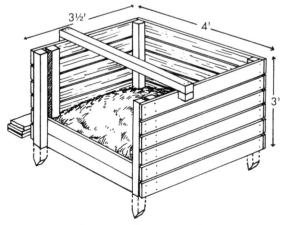

A homemade compost bin

Problems

OK, let's deal with difficulties you may have getting hot compost hot. (I've left this until now because, as I'm sure you've noticed, I just *hate* to start things off on a negative note.)

It stinks. I mean, the pile smells *rotten*. Well, it probably is rotting — that is, decomposing anaerobically. Why? It may be too wet. In that case, turn it, adding in some dry material as you go. It may be too full of fresh grass clippings, spoiled hay, or fall leaves, materials that tend to mat together. Turn the pile, breaking up the matted layers and, again, mixing in some dry material as you go. It may have too-large vegetable pieces — a plethora of kitchen scraps, possibly. Same solution: turn and mix in dry.

It stinks, but in a different way — namely, it has an *ammonia* smell. Too much nitrogen, my friend. Turn the pile and — guess what? — incorporate more brown matter.

It doesn't heat up. It may be too dry. If so, turn and wet. It could be too wet. If so, turn and dry (add some dry ingredients). It may be too squashed down. Turn and fluff.

Most likely, though, it's short on the hot sauce — Mr. Nitrogen. Turn the pile (we're always turning that pile, aren't we? Well, you have to get under the hood of a car to fix the engine, you know) and this time, incorporate more nitrogen-rich material — manure, legumes, blood meal, for example — as you do.

You don't have enough materials. Actually, in my opinion, this is most often the biggest problem with making compost at home. Unless you have fields and livestock, it's not likely you'll have enough materials on hand to make a very big compost pile.

One very effective solution is to turn part of your property into an alfalfa patch, and cut that greenery every time it gets to be 12–16 inches high. If you're not ready to create a home hayfield (call me crazy, but I *am* ready to), you'll have to forage or buy good compost ingredients. Anyone nearby with a stable? It's hard to beat livestock bedding. Food-processing plant down the road?

Truly Hot Compost

"Every garden book wants you to make a compost pile that gets good and hot, but you know what? You can overdo it.

"This happened years ago — I was *much* younger than I am today. I had a large garden with a compost heap. You know, the wire wrapped around four-stakes kind, filled with stuff like leaves and grass clippings and the like. Somewhere I'd heard that you could put woodstove ashes in your compost pile, so one day I dumped a bucket of that in.

"Well, I guess those ashes had one or two little sparks left in them. And the day was a little windy. About an hour or so later, I looked out the window and there were white clouds of smoke coming out of my compost! The dry grass in the pile hadn't burst into flame, but it was smoldering like crazy. I had to rush out and hose down my pile.

"It made my pile real small real fast. I guess that's what comes of letting your compost pile get a little too hot!"
— *Bill Novak, public relations coordinator for Fiskars, a garden cutting tool company based in Wausau, Wisconsin*

Perhaps you can round up buckwheat hulls, rice hulls, molasses residue, old hops, commercial fish scraps, feathers, and so on.

Eliot Coleman strongly recommends buying *straw* (grain stems after the grain has been harvested; hay still has the seeds in it). In fact, he calls straw "the best brown ingredient of all," and claims it almost *ensures* compost success. It breaks down quickly and cleanly. It's widely available. Best of all, it's hollow and very fluffy, so it's wonderful at incorporating air into a pile. Coleman even likes to make his compost bins out of stacked bales of straw. They insulate as well as support, and, after that batch is done, can be used as an ingredient in the next one. If you're nervous about goofing up with compost, I'd take Coleman's advice and start out using straw as your brown ingredient.

Commercial Composters

Speaking of bins, what about all those commercial composters you see advertised in gar-

den magazines and catalogs? Are they worth it? My opinion is . . . well . . . maybe not. Compost composts quickly and fumelessly when it gets hot. And a pile heats up better if it has at least a cubic yard of mass.

Many commercial composters do not hold three-foot cubes of material. To make them cook well, you need to add finely *shredded* ingredients in the right proportions, preferably all at one time. In other words, if you think you can just go out each night and toss in the day's chunks of garbage, give the contents a stir, and pull out a batch of fine, finished compost when you've finally filled the bin or barrel, you're probably going to be distinctly (get it?) disappointed. (I sure was.)

An Easy Way Out

Here's a neat trick: when you just want to recycle kitchen garbage or other small amounts of organic residue without going to all the trouble of incorporating them in a compost pile, try **trench composting.** Just dig a short trench in a pathway or other nongrowing area in your garden and bury the material. The next day you can just dig a little down the path to extend your trench and put in that day's residue. Such burying is a simple, in-place composting technique that works well on a small scale.

■ ■ ■ ■ ■

Speaking of burying, it's about time for this topic to R.I.P. We've spent the last two chapters on improving the soil in our gardens — and, as I'm sure you know by now, it's been a topic well worth the space and emphasis. But, hey, the best part about gardening (warning: wise words ahead) is *gardening*. So let's get back out there.

WOMAN DROWNS DAHLIA — But Dehydrates Daffodils!

Plants need water. Heck, plants are water: a tomato, for instance, is 93.5 percent water. But I'm not just talking about juicy fruits: the woody parts of a plant come from water, too. (They're made of carbohydrates — combinations of carbon and hydrogen — right? Well, plants get that carbon from the carbon dioxide in the air, but they get the hydrogen from good ol' H_2O.) Plants even get their dinner from water. (Roots don't eat dirt; they absorb nutrients in solution.)

I forgot to water my seedlings — and I KILLED them all!

So if you think you can grow a garden without watering, either you live in a very wet climate or — face it, bud — you're all dry. (At least your plants will be.)

Watering isn't hard. It can even be peaceful, a way to bless your plants gently at the start or end of the day. True, if you have to water a lot, it may cross the line from peaceful to monotonous at times. A West Coast gardener I know once said that dryland westerners (like him) feel about watering the way eastern gardeners (like me) feel about weeding — they have to do it so often that it becomes a burdensome chore. Well, sir, when it comes to chores, I'll take standing around with a hose to kneeling and pulling weeds any day.

A Good Question

"I'll tell you one garden mistake that seems common to nearly every house in the country. Why is there only one hose bib on a house, and it way at the back? What happens when you want to water a flowerbed at the front of your house? You know what happens? That hose wipes out entire beds of flowers, that's what happens!"

— Jeff Lowenfels, a newspaper and television garden authority in Anchorage, Alaska. Also a lawyer, this ardent gardener frequently refers to himself as "the dirtiest lawyer in America."

69

But, East, West, or in between, you can water efficiently instead of wastefully. You can use as little of this precious (and costly) resource as possible . . . and be as conserving of your own *time* as possible, as well.

You know, I don't think there's a Classic Gardener's Mistake for me to expose in the watering department (other than just plain *failing* to do it). Instead, there're a whole slew of little ways beginners can *mis*water, turning on the spigot when they think they should rather than when the plants actually need it. The difference between the experienced and beginner gardener thus is that the experienced gardener has learned when, how, and how much to water. He or she doesn't waste time — or water — but still gets the best results.

My job in this chapter is to share as many of these "wise waterer's" secrets as possible.

A rain gauge can help you gauge your garden's needs, but you should also dig down a few inches.

An Inch a Week?

One of the classic truisms you'll read in almost every gardening book is that your garden should receive an inch of water a week. That, fellow liquid lovers, is a *lot:* the equivalent of 62 gallons over a mere 10x10-foot square! More like a two-hour downpour than a friendly afternoon shower.

If you intend to stand out there with a hose spraying an inch of water over your whole garden every time that much moisture doesn't fall out of the skies, you *are* going to get tired of watering. You're also going to run up a heck of a water bill or run your well dry!

To put an inch of water on your garden every week would a) take a lot of time and b) cost a good bit of money. To be honest, I don't know a single inch-a-week amateur gardener. Here's how they avoid that and still grow lush gardens.

I killed with kindness — by overwatering. Even a tough old philodendron can get root rot!

Don't water when the garden doesn't need it. You can set up a rain gauge (store-bought or home rigged) in your garden to measure how much moisture your local sky has been donating. That's all to the good, but it's not the whole story. Different soils and slopes drain differently. More important is the question of how much water your *soil* (not your rain gauge) has received.

To learn that, **dig.** In all but wet weather, the surface of your garden will probably be dry. But when you dig down a few inches, the soil should feel moist. Squeeze a ball of it in your hand. Does it stay together? If so, good. If it flakes apart, it's probably watering time.

Look at your plants. Many plants may wilt some during the middle of a hot day. Large-leaved ones are particularly prone to showing a bit of nonserious wilting. But no plant should look wilted at the cooler beginning or end of a day. If it does, you need to water — now. Too much water stress and a plant will not recover.

For that matter, if a *lot* of plants look wilted during the heat of the day, I'd grab the hose and rush to put out the "fire." Many garden books don't recommend this: their authors claim that the beads of water left on plants in the hot sun will act like little magnifying glasses, so the leaves will get burned. I used to believe that, too, until I sat on the porch with my kids one hot summer day after a water fight. None of *us* got any magnifying burn marks. Why should plants? So I no longer worry about water burns on plants. I still don't think midday watering is a good idea in general — too much moisture will get lost to evaporation — but in an emergency, hose away.

Adapt your watering to your plants' needs. A bed of new seeds or freshly sprouted seedlings needs to stay constantly moist. If it even begins to dry out, the starts may die. So you'll probably need to water them once or even more a day. There's no point in watering them deeply, though. You have to keep the *surface* moist with those little guys; that's where their roots are.

Moist soil balls up.

A Dump Like This

"My wife, Katy, and I both graduated from Cornell with degrees in horticulture. After five years in the Army, we decided to buy a rundown greenhouse business. One of the flowers we planned to grow was snapdragons, so we ordered a quarter pound of seed from the George Ball Seed Company.

"They wrote back and said there wasn't that much seed in the country. The seed is so small that $\frac{1}{64}$th of an ounce is a good-sized purchase!

"I guess we realized then that college theory and hands-on horticulture are two different things!

"Still, we learned fast. In a few years, with our plants and weekly radio and newspaper columns and such, we'd become pretty well known. In those days, we changed the soil in the greenhouse every summer, a big, messy, and very hot job. I would run around in shorts — not even shaving for two or three days.

"A fellow came in with some weeds he wanted identified. 'I'm looking for the guy they call the Green Thumb,' he said.

" 'I'm the guy,' I replied.

" 'Seriously, I'm looking for Doc.'

" 'I am the guy.'

" 'Look, Mac, if you had half the brains that guy has, you wouldn't be working in a dump like this!'

"You know, at that particular moment, I wasn't 100 percent sure I disagreed."

— Doc and Katy Abraham,
"The Green Thumb" gardeners, who live
in Naples, New York, are authors of
Green Thumb Wisdom.

Conversely, bigger plants should be watered deeply. Their soil should get a thorough soaking to encourage their roots to grow deeply into the soil — where moisture is more likely to be constant — rather than spread shallowly just under the surface. To be honest, most of us don't have the patience to stand in a spot long enough to water it deeply. (Go ahead, test yourself. Water an area until you think you've gotten it thoroughly wet, then dig in that spot and see how little moisture has soaked in.) Even if you do, if you're using a hose, you're probably going to cause a miniature erosive surface flood, long before you soaked the lower soil well. A hose is just too rough an instrument.

When you want to water deeply, you're better off using a sprinkler or a drip-irrigation system. I'll cover drip irrigation in a bit. When it comes to sprinklers, I don't know of any special merits that one kind has over another: choose the kind you like. (However, by setting it up on a sawhorse or post rather than having it sit on the ground, you'll be able to water more evenly.)

Do consider getting a timer to put on your spigot. A simple one is inexpensive and can be set to run your sprinkler for as long or short as you want. It'll keep you from making my mistake: turning on the sprinkler and forgetting about it. More than once, I've drained my home's 500-gallon water reservoir before I realized that — oops! — I left the sprinkler on again!

By the way, to be fair, I should note that some authorities say you *can* water mature plants lightly — *if* you do it every day. I'm sure they're right; I just don't think it's a very practical idea for most we-sometimes-do-other-things-beside-garden people.

Water at the right time of day. Nobody recommends watering in the heat of the day

(unless you're facing crisis-stressed plants). It wastes too much water. Indeed, on a hot day, much of the water applied by a sprinkler can be lost to evaporation, a huge waste.

So most experienced gardeners advise watering in the morning or early evening. Which time is better? Depends on whom you talk to — or more accurately, where you live. Many eastern gardeners prefer morning. Why? Because they're leery of plant diseases, which are fostered by damp conditions.

To reduce disease problems, they water early, so the foliage will get a chance to dry out during

Drip irrigation puts water where plants need it, at their roots.

the day — rather than late, when the leaves would likely stay damp all night. They also try to work out ways to water at the base of plants, rather than overhead, to help keep those leaves as dry as possible. And they *never* work in their gardens when leaves are wet because at such times their activities are likely to spread disease from one plant to another.

Conversely, many western gardeners living in dryland conditions figure that their greenery has about as much chance of catching a plant disease as they do. They like to water at the end of the day because then the moisture will have all night to soak in, so the least possible amount of that precious resource will be lost to evaporation.

The solution? Choose which end of the day you water based on your local climate.

Mulch. You've heard this word from me before, haven't you? Mulch saves water. A surface layer covering your garden practically nixes evaporation loss and can greatly — repeat, *greatly* — reduce your plot's watering needs. If you're at all concerned about keeping up with your garden's watering needs, you're practically crazy not to do this.

Use drip irrigation. Once upon a time, an Israeli engineer, Syncha Blass, noticed how much better a tree grew near a leaky spigot he hadn't had time to fix. A flower bloomed over his head (you expected me to say, "A light went on"?), and drip irrigation was born.

Drip irrigation uses buried or ground-level hoses that let water out along their length. Some have small valves — **emitters** — spaced at various intervals; others, called **soaker hoses,** are built of a porous material that weeps moisture all along the hose.

Drip truly is wonderful. First off, it really saves water: it uses between one-third to one-half less water than normal overhead watering methods. (My garden sprinkler drains my home's 500-gallon reservoir in less than two hours. I can run my drip line all day and never run low on water.) It can increase growth, sometimes as much as doubling yields. And it reduces disease problems by putting water right where the plants need it — at their roots, not on their foliage.

However, drip irrigation can have some drawbacks. Two are minor. Drip lines can clog (to avoid this, put a small filter in your water-line at your spigot). And sunlight can degrade the lines over time (to avoid this, run your lines under mulch or underground).

Two other drawbacks are more significant. Drip lines need to be moved every time you replant. That's not a hassle with perennial flower beds, fruit trees, and perennial vegetables — just lay the line under the soil be-fore you plant, put in your plants and mulch, and then leave well enough alone. But it is an inconvenience with annual flowers or vegetable plantings.

Also, drip ain't cheap: a 50-foot drip line kit can go for $25.

Maybe there's a third drawback: I suspect some people are intimidated by drip, fearing it's as complicated as indoor plumbing. That's not so. Setting up a drip system ranks right up there with building alongside Tinker Toys; it's more fun than anything else.

I think the easiest way to deal with those last two considerations is to start small. Begin by trying drip in just one area of your garden. Or even just start with one line: I used to move one 25-foot soaker hose from row to row in my garden. I bet you'll find that drip irrigation is worth the cost and the installation effort. I certainly did.

A watering wand is helpful for evenly soaking the ground around a plant.

A soaker drip line

Other Tricks of the Trade

Let's end this watering chapter with a sampling of other water-saving tricks gardeners use.

- Punch a few holes in the bottom of a large can or plastic milk jug and set that in the ground next to water-loving plants. When you fill the container, the water will slowly seep into the soil near the plant's roots.
- If you live in a truly arid area, consider doing the opposite of raised-bed gardening: sunken-bed gardening. Plant in basins, so any water your plants get will stay right around the base of your plants.
- Wind can really suck the water out of plants, so use windbreaks to reduce evaporation losses. Plant on the downwind side of walls, trees, or fences.
- For those times when you need to stand by a section of soil with a hose, consider getting a watering wand, a piece of pipe with a many-holed headpiece at the bottom. It spreads the water evenly right near the ground.
- Lastly, don't skimp on hose. Buy the highest quality garden hose you can afford. I mean this. If you buy some cheap, easy-kinking, soon-leaking product, you will live to regret it. Guaranteed.

An in-ground milk jug waterer

Cucumber Pyramid Power

"You know how they say you're supposed to plant seeds like cucumbers and watermelons in hills? Well, when I started out, I didn't think they meant little clusters in a slightly raised mound. Heck, I thought they meant *real* hills!

"So I built virtual pyramids for my first cucumber seeds. What happened? They all dried right out, that's what happened!"
— *George Flynn, a gardener and schoolteacher in Newton, New Jersey*

A Letter
From a Down and Dirty Gardener

Dear Fellow Fallen Grower,

Do you want the "downright dirty stuff"? Illegal acts, politically incorrect gardening deeds, the things one confesses to one's priest? I have plenty of such confessions to atone for. I'll tell them to you, sure, but for only one reason: to help other gardeners who may feel alone with their shame. Maybe I should form a support group with an 800 number. Oh, and write a book on the subject! Heck, I'll put out a video!

Here you go . . .

I have sinned. I have sinned.

SIN #1

I have *deprived* my Easter cactus of food and water. Then around February I water and feed it. It begins to form buds, thinking this is its last chance to set seed. I feel no remorse for this deceit. I just want blooms for Easter.

SIN #2

I have *forced* bulbs!

SIN #3

I have *brutally pruned* my wisteria vine and cut out branching roots. I showed no mercy and, in fact, felt guilty satisfaction as I ripped it away from the security of my home's clapboards.

SIN #4

I have *gassed* two groundhogs. I hit one with a shovel. And I've cursed innocent rabbits and deer. (My children hate me for it.)

SIN #5

I have *stoned* potato beetles and grubs. That's what they used to do to witches in Salem.

SIN #6

I have overwatered my geraniums and *drowned* them. If that were done to people, I'd be in jail.

SIN #7

I have *left* my houseplants "Home Alone" for too long. Poor things.

SIN #8

I have done light and moisture *deprivation experiments* on bean plants in my classroom.

SIN #9

I have *mocked* the whole sacred process of germination by giving my children "Chia Pets."

SIN #10

I have *given liquor* to slugs. I'm sure they were underage.

SIN #11

And, worst of all (I hate to admit), there were many lost and misguided years in my youth when *I didn't compost.*

I have sinned. I have sinned.

*— By Deep Gardener, an anonymous source
(reported to us by famed horticultural investigative reporter
Katrina Nicke, who daylights as head of the Walt Nicke
Company, a fine mail-order garden tool company
based in Topsfield, Massachusetts)*

GARDEN RUNS WILD — Out of Control, Neighbors Say

Procrastination has its price: I couldn't see the flowers for the weeds!

There's an old folk song about the plight of farmers called "The Farmer Is the Man." Ever heard it? The first verse goes like this:

We worked through spring and summer,
The winter and the fall,
But the mortgage worked the hardest
And the steadiest of us all.
It worked on nights and Sundays.
It worked each holiday.
It settled down among us
And never went away.

All you have to do is substitute the word "weeds" for "mortgage" and it sums up the plight.

Weeds are an inevitable, sizable, seemingly never-ending part of gardening. Weeding, believe it or not, is so prominent an activity that there are schools of *philosophy* about it.

There's the *left-wing,* "horticulturally correct" branch of weed thinking, epitomized by Ralph Waldo Emerson, who said that weeds are just plants whose virtues have not yet been discovered. By this light, weeds are guardians of the soil, rushing in to bandage wounded ground. They're misunderstood, the right plants in the wrong place.

There's the *right-wing,* "horticulturally incorrect" branch of weed thinking that goes something like: "Weeds are genetically bred to invade. The more you chop them, the more they spread. Worse yet, they're all illegal immigrants. Dandelions, crabgrass, clover, pigweed, lamb's-quarter, buttercup, mullein, plantain, yarrow — not one of them grew here before the Pilgrims arrived." By this light, weeds are vega-villains, killer bees of the garden, especially developed to take over disturbed soil.

There's even a *philosophical* branch of philosophical weed thinking, well expressed by Patricia Thorpe in an essay she once wrote for *House and Garden.* "Weeding is the active heart of gardening," she wrote. "Garden design, plant selection, even the planting itself are just forms of garden theory — how you imagine your garden to be. Weeding is the day-by-day realization of that garden, fulfilling your

The big secret? Get 'em while they're small.

original aspirations, changing them, giving them up for new dreams." By this light, weeds are doing us a favor, forcing us into close relationship with our gardens.

My own conclusion from all these weedy ruminations is simply this: no matter what kind of thinking people favor, they've obviously got weeds to cope with. Weeds are in everyone's garden. In fact, I figure the reason there is so much reflective thinking about weeding is that everybody's got *lots* of time to reflect . . . while they're weeding! I guess that's my cue to get to work on some of my own worthwhile weeding words.

The One, The True, The Only Secret of Weeding

I'll be giving you lots of practical weed-beating tips in this chapter, but I might as well start out with THE BIG ONE. You ready? There is

One and Only One Secret to successful weeding: **get 'em while they're small.** The old Chicago politicians used to say, "Vote early and vote often!" That's the trick here: "weed early and weed often!"

Eliot Coleman put the thought more eloquently in his terrific book, *The New Organic Grower:* "Too many growers consider hoeing to be a treatment for weeds, and thus they start too late. Hoeing should be understood as a means of prevention. Don't weed, cultivate. *Cultivation* is the shallow stirring of the surface soil in order to cut off small weeds and prevent the appearance of new ones. *Weeding* is when the weeds are already established. Cultivation deals with weeds before they become a problem. Weeding deals with the problem after it has occurred."

In other words, there is only one Classic Mistake with Weeds: **failing to keep ahead of them.**

The rest is just details.

Why

Why is keeping up with weeds so important? Two reasons. First, weeding is a snap when weeds are small — but it's a royal pain when they're big. And the vast majority of us don't like to do hard things. Plus, when you get behind on weeding, you can get so overwhelmed by how much weeding there is to do that you're tempted to just throw in the trowel and quit. (Don't; you'll never find that trowel again!) The by-far-the-best way to avoid that kind of humbling horticultural defeat is never to let the possibility of it arise.

Second, big weeds spread, either underground by runners or overland by seed. A single lamb's-quarter plant can bear thousands upon thousands of weed seeds, all ready to make your garden more weed-choked next year than it was

this. There's an old saying: one year's seeds equals seven years' weeds. Let this year's weeds go to seed and you'll be pulling their progeny for years to come.

How

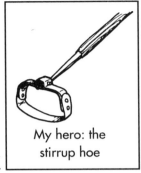

My hero: the stirrup hoe

To my way of thinking, there's one great tool for small-plant weeding: the **stirrup hoe.** You remember this fellow? I praised it back in Chapter 3. Also called the scuffle, oscillating, or Dutch hoe, it cuts right under the surface of the soil on both push or pull strokes. It's almost like *sweeping* the soil rather than chopping at it. Indeed, if you hold it with

Thumbs-up hoeing is easier on your back

your thumbs up, the way you do a broom, instead of thumbs down — the way most people hold a hoe — you'll be able to stand more erect while you work and thus greatly reduce any back pain.

A lot of gardeners — not just me — swear by the stirrup hoe. In fact, many market gardeners, people who have to keep *acres* of crops to keep under control, use wheel stirrup hoes, a tool that looks like an old horse-drawn plow except it has a wheel where the horse used to be and a stirrup hoe where the plow was.

When

When should you stirrup-hoe your garden? **Before it needs it!** Most annual weed seeds germinate in the top ¼-inch of soil. They're the ones who've gotten high enough up to reach the light. Whenever you till or dig a garden, you bring gobs of eager weed seeds into the sprouting zone. That's why I stressed the point, chapters earlier, that you should always cultivate the soil just before you plant in it. Use that stirrup hoe (or tiller if you set it to run shallowly across the soil) to cut off weeds you don't yet see that are already swelling or sprouting.

Hoe the area again around 10 days later because by then a new batch of weeds will be angling for sunlight. Some well-known gardeners will run over the garden with a rake at that time to get those weeds on the rise. And I mean run over — they'll rake right over a seedbed, on the idea that they're thinning their planting as well as getting early-bird weeds.

In another 10 to 14 days, hoe it again. Then again and again and — you'll have to cultivate four or five times before you have most of those weeds under control.

Meanwhile, inevitably, some weeds will have sprouted right among your crop or

Well, It Repelled Something!

"Back in 1971, my wife Ellen and I grew our first large-scale vegetable truck garden. It was completely organic. I used lots of compost and interspersed marigold seeds all around to repel insect pests.

"Soon all these little plants came up. We thought they were marigolds and left them alone. After all, they had hairy stems — they *looked* like marigolds. We were pleased as punch.

"By the middle of the summer, Ellen couldn't even go out into the garden anymore, she was sneezing so bad. You see, we had carefully cultivated an entire half-acre of thoroughly interplanted ragweed!"
— *Agricultural Consultant Bill Wolf of Salem, Virginia, a prominent advocate of organic agriculture and the head of Wolf Associates.*

flowers, where you can't reach them with a hoe. Those, alas, you'll need to pull by hand. They come out easier if the soil's moist. (However, you don't want to weed when plants are wet because your activities may spread plant disease.) But since some weeds keep a firmer grip on ol' *terra firma* than others, you may need to keep a trowel with you to completely root out the tough ones.

And, oh, one more thing: a stirrup hoe is pretty much ineffective on larger weeds. If you do let an area get ahead of you, you'll have to hack 'em back with a regular flat-blade hoe. Do be sure to sharpen the cutting edge of that hoe occasionally with a flat file (see page 22). It truly can make your work only half as hard. And at up to 2,000 chops per hour, that'll become a very noticeable difference.

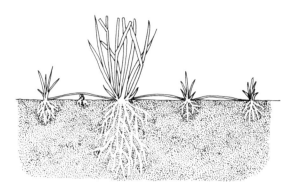

Perennial weeds have big taproots or spread by stolons or runners.

Perennial Villains

So far, I've been talking about **annual weeds**, one-year wonders that shoot up from seeds — lots and lots of seeds. They're not hard to weed (if you get them small). There are just so many of them in most soils that you have to go after them again and again and again.

But there's a whole other class of villain: **perennial weeds.** These multi-weaponed garden wreckers can sprout from seed, but they can also draw on stored energy in their root reserves or spread by underground runners, called stolons. Chopping a perennial weed just once will not do the job. In fact, rototilling an area with a runner-spread perennial weed can just make the problem *worse* by creating a whole bunch of little cuttings, each of which can sprout into a new plant!

A rogue's gallery of perennial villains would include such foliage felons as quackgrass, bindweed, burdock, dandelions, Canada thistle, and Johnson grass. How do you rein in such rascals?

Well, you can try to **wear them out.** If you keep them from ever getting more than half an inch high, eventually their roots will run out of reserves. So hoe, hoe, hoe and they'll just go.

Of course, let them get a little taller just one time and they'll restock their roots with energy — and you'll be back where you started.

You can try to **cover up perennial weeds.** Lay down black plastic or a very thick mulch for a year (pull any weeds that somehow still get up) and that should eliminate the problem. Since most of us don't want to give up our whole gardens for a year, you could do this section by section until you have unperennialed the entire garden.

Or you could do the **smother strategy** I mentioned when I talked about cover crops (Chapter 8). Remember? Start the spring with a thick planting of annual rye. When the date of your last expected spring frost passes, till under the rye and plant buckwheat — thickly, up to 4 pounds per 1,000 square feet. Till under and replant buckwheat every month until fall, then put in another rye crop. Next spring your soil should be perennial-weed free and of better quality to boot. Again, you'd probably want to do this to one section of your

Sadder but Wiser

"We occasionally use weed killers around some of our ornamental plants. And we have made some sad mistakes with those. At times, we haven't used enough, so the chemical didn't kill any weeds. Worse, other times we weren't careful enough and killed plants we were trying to grow. I remember with sadness the time we wiped out our phlox and young lilacs like crazy. Be very careful with weed killers."

— *Lewis Hill of Greensboro, Vermont. Lewis is the author of a number of fine gardening books, including the classic* Pruning Simplified.

garden at a time so you wouldn't lose a whole year of gardening.

Is It Worth It?

Does consistent, persistent, insistent diligence with weeding pay off? Yes. Gardeners who continually keep on top of their weeds end up with fewer and fewer new weeds every year. Eventually their soil becomes relatively clean and almost easy to take care of. So, yes, there is a pot of gold (or relatively weed-free soil, anyway) at the end of the diligent weeder's rainbow.

Other Tips on Weeds

- Don't be fooled by the fact that it's easy to keep up with weeds early in the season. Anybody can weed well in spring — the pest plants don't grow quickly then. Once the weather really warms up, though, weed growth increases sharply — at a rate that still surprises me every single year.
- Don't forget the M word. The more you mulch, the less you'll have to W.
- If your soil is fertile enough to grow crops or flowers closely together, their leaves will overlap as they mature and create a "living mulch" that partly shades out weeds.
- Don't forget to weed after your harvest. At the end of the year, weeds rush to make seed. You really have to keep on top of even small ones then if you don't want them sowing future weed crops on you.
- If you don't want to risk introducing weeds into your soil, don't mulch with hay (grass plants with seeds). Instead, use clean straw (grass plant stems after the seeds have been harvested). Also, don't add fresh (seed-filled) animal manure directly to the garden. Compost it *thoroughly* first.
- In general, a good time to do a cultivating

weeding is soon after a rain (as long as your plant leaves aren't wet). Water makes weeds sprout, you know.

- Consider reclassifying chickweed. You may have *Stellaria media,* a ground-hugging, fast-spreading weed in your garden. If so, think about *letting* it grow. "Excuse me," you're thinking, "let a weed *grow*?" Here's my experience. Chickweed sprouts in fall, spreads over winter, and dies back the middle of the following spring. Sounds like a nice winter cover crop to me!
- If you want to keep lawn weeds like crabgrass from migrating into your garden, "moat" your plot somehow. You could rototill around it periodically. You could dig an eight-inch-deep trench and fill that with bark chips. You could put in a wall of buried-on-end bricks. Or you could install a commercial edging. Take your pick.

Just for Mom

"The worst thing I ever did was to plant alstromeria, also called Peruvian lily, in my mother's garden. It's a lovely flower — I thought I was doing her a favor. But it's taken over everything.

"The plant has these little white tubers that multiply and spread like crazy. And they're eight inches down, so you can't dig them out. It wouldn't have become a problem if we lived in a colder area where the ground freezes in winter or if I'd planted a modern, not older variety.

"As it is, nowadays I go down to my mother's twice a year — to prune her fruit trees and dig out her alstromerias!"
— *Wendy Krupnick, a plant evaluator for Shepherd's Seeds in Felton, California.*

Chickweed: not bad after all?

■ Some people think you should weed during the heat of the day to be sure the plants you yank or chop will wilt instead of reroot. Some people weed in the morning or evening because they tend to wilt in the heat of the day themselves. And a few people weed at night. At night?! Yep, turns out that many weed seeds won't germinate without a brief exposure to sunlight, so cultivating the ground three hours or later after sunset can reduce weed germination by as much 70 percent! Of course, you'll have to wear a miner's lamp to see what

Voluminous Volunteers

"Every summer I find that some of my most enjoyable and colorful garden companions are volunteers, uninvited but very welcome plants that pop up right where Ma Nature sowed them the year before when my back was turned. But . . .

"One year when I had a small plot in a community garden, I visited my ground in May. I was surprised and pleased to see that many of the day-neutral strawberries I'd planted eleven months earlier had survived the garden's annual disk harrowing and, although a little disheveled, were greening up beautifully. That got me looking and, sure enough, clumps of the phlox, dianthus, and stokesia I had planted the year before were also poking through the debris. Then, near the garden's shed, I found a little catnip plant thrown by the harrow onto the bank. I gayly put the little minty plant in my plot.

"As the weeks went by and I sowed spinach, lettuce, carrots, and beets, more volunteers appeared. Everywhere I stepped,

there were dill seedlings, and tiny tomatoes with oddly shaped leaves. A tomatillo snaked its way around the young broccoli.

"Well, you probably know what happened next. I went away for a summer vacation and came back to find that not weeds, but *volunteers,* were taking over my garden. Dill heads were so big they leaned over into my neighbor's plot. The tomatoes were everywhere — in the carrots, the spinach, the strawberries. Indeed, cherry tomato vines had become the warp in the weave of my garden tapestry. Did I mention strawberries? They were busy becoming a lovely, nonfruiting ground cover. And the catnip? Don't ask.

"I had let the forces of nature totally overwhelm me and my garden. Worse, I guess you could say I had *volunteered* for the disaster!"

— *Barbara Richardson, who works for Gardeners Supply Company in Burlington, Vermont.*

you're doing, but don't worry. That little bit of light won't sprout anything.

■ Lastly, if you can't beat 'em, eat 'em! Many weeds are good for you! This isn't too surprising when you think about the fact that, in general, leaf crops are the most nutritious crops you can eat. (Example: broccoli leaves are more nutritious than broccoli heads!). So as long as you know what you're pulling, consider putting it on the plate, not the compost pile.

Purslane, for example, can be added to soups or salads, or munched on the spot. And it's loaded with vitamin C, beta-carotene, vitamin E, and omega-3 fatty acids. Lamb's-quarter is a classic forager's green. Cook it as you would a cultivated green or add young leaves to salads. Chicory, winter cress, dandelion, evening primrose, garlic mustard, rocket, wild garlic, shepherd's purse — there's a whole smorgasbord out there, growing for free. The trick? Pick 'em young. Many of them can get a little too tough or strong flavored as they mature.

■ ■ ■ ■ ■

Well, that's about all the weedy advice I have to share. Too bad in a way. I've always found talking (or writing) about weeding easier than doing it. And the more time I've been able to spend working on the words in this chapter, the longer I could put off working on the weeds in my own garden!

GARDENERS ENGAGE
in Slug Fest
(Slugs Win!)

"If you grow it, they will come."

Yes, they will. Sooner or later (probably sooner), when you start a garden, you'll have to deal with invasive pests. You'll be bugged by bugs.

What to do? The knee-jerk reaction is to reach for the quick fix: rush to the garden center, buy the strongest pesticide you can find, and launch an aerial invasion of your garden with sprays or dusts.

I sprayed first and asked questions later!

I would argue that that's a mistake. A common mistake, an understandable mistake — but a mistake, nonetheless.

Why? Before I answer that question, let me throw in a few prefatory words. Last chapter, we discussed the two opposing gardeners' opinions on weeds. Well, there are two opposing ideological camps on insect pests, too, only they aren't so much fun to talk about: people take their pest control beliefs seriously.

Obviously, I'm referring to organic vs. chemical pest control. It's not my goal here to offend supporters of either camp in this chapter, nor my intent to get up on a high soapbox and preach environmental moralism. Still, I'm not going to try to hide, either. I lean toward organic controls and practices, and I should share the reasons I do.

Why does Stone think reaching for a quick-fix toxic pesticide is a mistake? Or, to put the

First, Remove the Slugs

"Do you know what happened the day I learned that salt kills slugs? I rushed out and gleefully dissolved every slimy gastropod that was climbing over my lettuce plants. The next morning, I went outside — to discover that I'd killed all my lettuce, as well!"

— *Stan Peto, an anagram version of the name of a gardener from Fairview, North Carolina, who is otherwise too embarrassed to admit to ever having made any mistakes*

question in larger terms, why does he claim organic pest control is better than chemical pest control?

Well, it's not because I think chemical sprays don't work. Heck, no, they can be highly effective. Just look at that overflowing produce section in your local supermarket. Chemical agriculture — American agriculture — puts food on millions and millions of tables.

But you and I aren't operating large-scale American agribiz farms here, are we? We're growing home gardens. We're puttering around outside in the evening, nurturing fresh food and bright blooms because we want to. We find gardening fun, satisfying, rewarding — a life-creating activity that nurtures us as well as our plants. Well, sorry, I just don't see how spraying highly toxic — that is, deadly — poisons is compatible with all that. And I'm betting the first time you nervously don a face mask and long gloves to mix up and broadcast and clean up and dispose of a good strong batch of chemical brew, you'll start thinking the same thing yourself.

There are, of course, other reasons not to rely on chemical pesticides. Most of them are broad-spectrum killers, which means they attack both useful bugs (and other creatures) as well as pest ones. They can have harmful effects on groundwater, food, people, pets, and so on. In the long run, pests generally evolve resistance to them. And chemical sprays often attack the symptoms of a problem (the pest) rather than the cause (a growing practice you could improve).

You can learn more about these arguments on your own, if you wish. As I said, I'm not here to preach. I just felt it was only fair, going into this chapter, to give you a little basis for the organic pest-control approach I'll be taking.

A "-Cide" Story

"I forgot to label my containers of herbicides, pesticides, etc. Several years ago I THOUGHT I was applying bug spray to my vegetable garden, but instead sprayed everything with weed killer! A TOTAL DISASTER!"

— *A charter member of Oversprayers Anonymous, Anytown, USA.*

Axioms for Organics

Axiom 1: A little damage is OK. You and I have a big advantage over the commercial farmer: we don't have to raise picture-perfect produce or completely unblemished blooms. Our plants can sustain minor or moderate damage, and there's still plenty left for us to enjoy.

Consequently, we don't need to get rid of every bad bug; we just need to manage the situation so they don't inflict unacceptable damage.

Axiom 2: Healthy plants resist insects and disease. This is probably the Great Credo of Organics. I don't know if there's a secret organic gardener's handshake, but there sure is a club motto, and this is it. As Thomas Jefferson, a founding father (of our nation, not the Secret Organic Gardeners Society), wrote two hundred years ago to a friend, "I suspect that the insects which have harassed you have been encouraged by the feebleness of your plants; and that has been produced by the lean state of your soil."

The concept is simple: the winter my mother died, I had a big problem at work, my son's basketball team (which *I* was coaching) suddenly went from winning all its games to losing six in a row, and, to top it all off, I learned I needed more than $2,000 worth of dental work. So guess what? I got sick! Indeed, I was the only person in my family who got laid up by a visiting flu epidemic.

Why? Stress. Plants feel it, too. When plants are exposed to such conditions as cold weather, lack of water, or excess wind, they produce glutathione, an amino acid that helps shield them from environmental stress. The trouble is that some insects find glutathione-rich plants tastier than normal ones.

So do what you can to put your crops at ease. Don't set them out too early in the grow-ing season. Keep them well watered. Shield them from extreme cold and wind with cold frames, floating row covers, or windbreaks. Give them the right amounts of compost and organic fertilizers. All in all, learn what conditions your plants like best, and then try to provide them. (You know what the pop plant psychologists say — "A happy plant is a healthy plant.")

Many, many gardeners have observed this principle in practice: sometimes the flea beetles will attack one broccoli transplant (the one with damaged roots) and leave the one right beside it alone. And there's plenty of research to support it. To quote just one

---

Pest Profile

Colorado Potato Beetle

Description: Adult: ⅓-inch-long round beetle with black-and-yellow striped body. Larva: plump yellow-orange, soft-bodied insect with black head and a double row of black spots down the sides.

Controls:
- Handpick.
- Interplant potatoes with green beans.
- Plant horseradish, aromatic marigolds, or garlic as repellent plants.
- Use the B.T. strain for Colorado po-tato beetles.
- Dust damp foliage with wheat bran (it's supposed to swell — fatally — inside the larvae.
- Sprinkle diatomaceous earth.
- Spray pyrethrum.

Pest Profile

Aphid

wingless

winged

Description: ¹/₁₀-inch tear-shaped, soft-bodied insect, most often in green, but available in white, black, red, and other colors.

Controls:
- Plant nasturtiums, alliums, petunias, anise, coriander, or garlic as repellents.
- Raise healthy plants (aphids love weak or imbalanced ones, especially ones raised with too much nitrogen).
- Clean up plant residue.
- Spray water on tops and bottoms of leaves.
- Hang yellow sticky traps.
- Spray dishwashing soap, insecticidal soap, or horticultural oil spray.
- Sprinkle diatomaceous earth.

study, researchers at Cornell University found that "significantly smaller pest-insect populations are associated with the use of organic fertilizers relative to controls fertilized with highly soluble N-P-K materials or left unfertilized, at least for the particular experiment situation studied."

This is what I meant earlier about tackling the cause of a pest problem rather than the symptom. Many times if you can figure out better ways to raise a plant that has a persistent pest problem, you can reduce or eliminate the problem. (Some organic gardeners think that this holds true for every pest problem; I don't know about that.) Indeed, pests and diseases have been called the best professors of agriculture because they challenge gardeners to learn ways to raise their plants to avoid them.

Axiom 3: Garden as a whole system. The more you look at your whole garden as a living biological unit, the more you can learn ways to make it mutually self-supporting. The most obvious example of this is finding ways to encourage toads, birds, beneficial insects, and the like — creatures that thrive on your plot's pests — to frequent your garden.

Axiom 4: Know your enemy. Identify the creature that's causing the damage; then learn about it. The more you know about a pest, the easier it is to find its weak point. After all, different solutions work better for different pests
.

Axiom 5: Don't use chemical powder, use brain power. Sharp observation, controlled experimentation, outwitting those six-legged varmints — these are our best weapons.

Speaking of brains, let's get down to some . . .

General Tactics

Basic preventive measures are your best approach to pest problems.

Time Your Plantings

In most areas, many problem pests reach their peak populations about the same time every year. If you know when that time will likely occur, you can often plan to harvest before that date or to plant after it. For instance, in parts of the Northeast, the biggest flush of cabbage root maggots hatches out around two weeks before the last frost date. A mere fortnight later, they are hardly a problem.

The trick here, of course, is knowing when pest peaks are. A local agricultural extension agent should have this information for your

Pest Profile

Mexican Bean Beetle

Description: Adult: 1/3-inch-long round beetle with 16 black spots on orangish wings (like an orange ladybug). Larva: 1/3-inch, soft-bodied yellow insect with little spinelike growths.
Controls:
- Handpick.
- Interplant green beans with potatoes.
- Plant garlic as a repellent crop.
- Time plantings to miss peak outbreaks.
- Clean up garden debris to eliminate their winter home.
- Sprinkle diatomaceous earth to kill larvae.
- Spray pyrethrum.

area. You can also discover the patterns for yourself by starting to track the pest outbreaks in your garden. Timed plantings are simple defense measures that cost nothing, but can be one of the most effective ways to avoid insect problems.

Grow Resistant Varieties

Certain plant varieties are less susceptible to insect and disease damage than others. (For instance, thick-skinned tomatoes, tiny-haired bean plants, glossy- or purple-leaved brassicas, tight-husked corn, and multirooting squashes succumb less to their most common pests than do other cultivars of the same plants.) Most seed catalogs will point out their *disease*-resistant cultivars. *Insect* resistance is harder to learn about.

Check with your local county agricultural extension service, which should also know what pests are most prominent in your area. Keep up with the latest discoveries related in garden magazines. And plant more than one variety of a crop in your garden and see if some have better pest resistance.

Use Companion Planting

Companion planting — now there's a topic both of good gardening common sense *and* (let's be honest) a lot of organic hooey.

Companion planting is essentially a good idea. The more diversified the plantings in a garden the less likely you'll have insect problems. After all, the jumble of sight and scent signals makes it harder for specific pests to locate their preferred foods. Large plantings of a single crop, on the other hand, practically scream: "Come and get it!"

Hooey-wise, though, there's a seemingly infinite number of plant matchmakers declaring which crops do and do not like growing next to each other . . . and a lot of the combinations seem to have a tenuous basis in fact. Don't believe every plant partnership you read about. Still, there *are* pairings that have found some confirmation in research. Clover interplanted with broccoli has been shown to deter flea beetles. Onions do repel rust flies from nearby carrots. Broccoli reduces the number of striped cucumber beetles on companion cucumbers. Tomatoes lessen the number of diamondback moth larvae on adjacent cabbage. Aromatic marigolds reduce the number of problem nematodes on the roots of nearby crops.

Other pairings that may not have much research backing have been observed by so

Pest Profile

Cucumber Beetles

Description: ¼-inch greenish yellow, thin beetle with a black head and either about a dozen spots (the spotted cucumber beetle) or a few stripes (the striped CB) down its back.
Controls:
- Heavy mulching.
- Handpick (check the undersides of leaves).
- Strew onion skins as a deterrent.
- Time plantings to avoid peak infestations.
- Spray a mix of wood ashes and hydrated lime.
- Spray a mix of hot pepper, garlic, and water.
- Spray pyrethrum.

many organic growers, so the odds are good that they work. Chives, onions, and garlic — for obvious reasons — do seem to repel pests that are trying to *smell* their way to other crops. The legendary interplanting of green beans and potatoes does seem to reduce both Mexican bean beetle and Colorado potato beetle infestations.

Once again, there's room for your own observations and discoveries. Last year I heard about a gardener who swears that dill plants chased Mexican bean beetles out of her bean patch. Those bean-chewing varmints are a major pest in my own garden, so you can bet I'm going to try that pairing this summer and see for myself if it works!

Pest Profile

Slugs and Snails

Description: You know what a snail looks like. A slug looks the same — without the shell. (And, yes, they're not insects, but, boy, do they cause problems.)

Controls:

- Handpick (especially by flashlight at night).
- Set out ground-level saucers of beer for them to drown themselves in.
- Set out boards, cabbage leaves, grapefruit rinds, or other objects for them to hide under at night. You can find — and destroy — them easily the next day.
- Create a rough barrier of gravel, seaweed mulch, cedar or oak bark, or crushed eggshells they have to cross.
- Surround garden with boards set at a 45° angle, their undersides coated with petroleum jelly.
- Use commercially available (but expensive) copper barriers.
- Sprinkle diatomaceous earth.

Rotate Crops

We've talked about this before because rotating crops (never planting a crop in the same place two years in a row) improves soil fertility. But it also has pest advantages. As biointensive gardening expert John Jeavons put it, "Crop rotation is a way of companion planting over time." Many insects lay their eggs or overwinter near their favorite crop. If they emerge the next season to find something different growing there, they'll be that much less likely to cause damage.

Mulch

Yep, that's right, our old friend Mr. Mulch is back again. Mulching a garden can often improve growing conditions by reducing temperature and water fluctuations. More than one gardener has told me of times that putting a hay mulch around a crop clearly reduced its pest problems.

Actually, though, mulching can both help reduce or *create* pest problems. That nice moist shelter can comfortably harbor snails, slugs, earwigs, and pillbugs. On the other hand, it can promote the presence of beneficial creatures. An agricultural researcher in Tennessee recently found a dramatic increase in spiders (major good guys in the garden) and from 60 to 70 percent less plant damage when she compared mulched first-year gardens to unmulched ones.

Then, too, mulch can sometimes create a *physical* pest deterrent. A Virginia Polytechnic Institute scientist, for instance, observed that a good layer of wheat straw or grass hay around potato plants reduced damage from Colorado potato beetles.

It's up to you, then, to observe what happens when you mulch various plants and assess whether the overall effect is positive or negative.

Clean Up the Plot

Many pests like to lay eggs or overwinter in decaying garden litter. Some good examples are asparagus beetles, corn borers, flea beetles, leafhoppers, Mexican bean beetles, squash bugs, and tarnished plant bugs. So clean up old leaves, vines, stalks, and fruits each fall — especially from heavily infested crops — and compost or burn them. Interrupting the life cycle of such pests can significantly reduce your problem. Be sure to do a thorough cleanup. To get all the corn borers, for instance, you need to pull all your old corn plants, leaving no more than one inch in the ground.

Cultivate

Digging or tilling up the soil in late fall or early spring can expose underground grubs, eggs, and pupae to hungry birds and cold. This will interrupt the pests' life cycle and can be an excellent way to reduce the next year's infestation. Cutworms, carrot rust flies, grasshoppers, hornworms, cabbageworms, Japanese beetles, leaf miners, and wireworms are all pests that can be reduced with this tactic.

I didn't keep picking the Japanese beetles — and, as a result, didn't get to keep picking any roses, either!

Inspect New Plants

Don't import pests or disease with that must-buy bush or broccoli you just purchased. Give it a careful going-over, or even a quarantine period, to make sure you don't add

Cleaning up the garden at the end of the season will destroy many pests' winter homes.

much, much more than you bargained for to your garden

Going on the Offense

"Enough wise words of generic preventative goodness!" you cry. "I've done all those things (OK, I didn't, but I promise I will next year). But there're still bugs bugging me garden right now, mate. What'll I do?"

Ah, so you want aggressive, interventive, *attack* measures! Why didn't you say so?!

Handpick 'Em

It's old. It's slow. It works. Carry a bucket or can with some water and perhaps a bit of gasoline or kerosene, and meander around the plants, shaking the bad guys into your container. Handpicking works best 1) early in the season, before the bugs have had time to be fruitful and multiply, and 2) early in the day, when many of them are still lethargic. Japanese beetles, in particular, are slow starters while the dew is still a'weighin' on their wings.

I pay my kids a penny a bug, which may not sound like much, but adds up into dollars satisfyingly (for them) quickly.

Barricade 'Em

I love this one. Simply block their approach. It's simple, it works, and it's great fun imagining those six-legged varmints futilely knocking on the barrier trying to get in.

A couple of classic examples are **cutworm** and **root maggot collars.** Many a gardener has cut circles out of cardboard or cups and put them around the base of all their spring broccoli, cabbage, and cauliflower plants to keep cutworms from toppling the young transplants. Likewise, laying a sheet of tarpaper (or a thick pile of ashes) around the

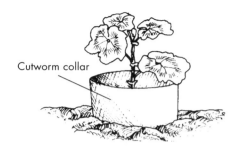

Cutworm collar

Keep cutworms at bay with a cardboard collar.

base of those brassicas keeps the cabbage fly from laying the eggs that turn into subterranean, root-chomping maggots.

The barricade receiving the most attention these days (all of it richly deserved) is the **floating row cover,** that white, wispy plant blanket you see in all the gardening supply catalogs. While it's often promoted as providing a few degrees of frost protection, it's even better as a pest barrier. Lay it over any young plant that gets chewed and then the chewers can't get to it. Got flea beetles on your eggplants? Cabbage worms on your broccoli? Rust flies on your carrots? You name it; if it doesn't come out of the ground immediately below, row covers block it.

Drawbacks? Minor. Fertilizing insects can't get in, either — to do their pollination thing — and some plants can overheat under row covers in the middle of summer. Most people use row covers on young, vulnerable crops to help them start well so they'll be big enough to withstand some pest damage and then take them off before heat wave and pollination time.

Trap 'Em

You know those steel-toothed, jaw-shaped, leg-chomping hunter's traps that are always springing shut on innocent creatures in the movies? Well, you won't be using those here. I'm talking about such traps as white or yel-

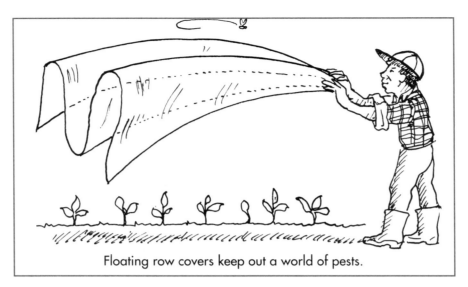

Floating row covers keep out a world of pests.

low squares coated with a sticky substance like Tanglefoot (these work well on tiny, flighty pests) or sticky red balls hung in fruit trees or even commercial pheromone (smell-hormone) traps hung to lure bad bugs to their doom. Don't leave these out all the time — just set them out to deal with a specific problem.

Actually, the popular Japanese beetle pheromone traps work so well they may attract more JB's to your garden than you had before. Set them a ways *upwind* of your plot to lure the invaders away from it.

Another form of plant trap is the **trap crop:** lure them away by growing something they like even more than what you're really after to lure them away. For instance, grow bok choy as well as eggplants. When the flea beetles all flock to the bok choy, you can pull them up and dispose of the bugs.

Counterattack, Part I

Enlist the help of beneficial insects. There are more than one million insect species in the world, and only about one-tenth of one percent of them are pests. Many of the rest are pests to the pests. On the facing page are just a few of the common, naturally occurring beneficial insects.

Get the picture? Armies of six-legged allies are available. How do you get them to work in your garden? (**1**) ***Don't ever* spray with broad-spectrum pesticides,** thereby knocking

A Few Beneficial Insects

Spined soldier beetles:
attack cabbage loopers, cabbageworms, Mexican bean beetles.

Lacewings: attack aphids.

Predatory mites: attack pest mites.

Ground beetles: attack caterpillars, cutworms, and other soft-bodied larvae.

Australian lady beetles:
attack mealybugs.

Ichneumon wasps: attack caterpillars and borers.

Braconid wasps: attack aphids, hornworms, cutworms, cabbageworms, tent caterpillars, and more.

Assassin bugs: attack aphids, caterpillars, Colorado potato beetles, Japanese beetles, leafhoppers, Mexican bean beetles, and more.

Ladybugs: attack aphids, rootworms, whiteflies, chinch bugs, Colorado potato beetles, mealybugs, scales, and spider mites.

Trichogramma wasps: attack cutworms, armyworms, cabbage loopers, hornworms, corn borers, codling moths, fruitworms, leafworms, and more.

out the good guys with the bad. And **(2) create the kind of environment they like.** By this I mean, grow plants they (sometimes in one particular stage of development) like to feed on. What plants are those?

Umbelliferae (parsley family) are a favorite of parasitic wasps. This group includes dill, caraway, angelica, lovage, Queen Anne's lace, and sweet fennel. (By the way, most parasitic wasps are so tiny you can hardly see them — you don't have to worry about them stinging *you*.)

Compositae (composite family), such as tansy, cosmos, anthemis, and aromatic marigolds, lure in ladybugs, small wasps, lacewings, and more.

Cover crops — now there's something else you've heard me mention before. But in truth, many cover crops do attract beneficial insects. Buckwheat, crimson clover, white clover, vetch, and alfalfa all pull in beneficials. Some gardeners will cut down only half a cover crop at a time and plant their vegetables or flowers next to the still-standing cover. That practically invites the good bugs to come on over and find the bad ones.

Mail-order bugs. What about importing beneficial bugs — buying them from mail-order companies? My own opinion: it's tricky. You have to time it perfectly so that the predator arrives exactly when the prey is at the right population and the right stage of development. Then, unless you have an ongoing supply of prey bugs and other necessities of beneficial bug life, they'll probably die out or leave after dealing with that one infestation. I'd recommend making your own garden more conducive to the beneficials you can lure in naturally.

Counterattack, Part II

Robins, finches, chickadees, starlings, wrens, sparrows, warblers, bats, toads, and even snakes are all happy to gobble up gobs of garden pests. How do you attract them? Raise a variety of plants, and (very important) provide them a water source in your garden.

Bring Out the Guns

Do you get the feeling I've been putting off, almost avoiding, the topic of organic pesticides? You're absolutely right — because that's what *you* should do. Always try the mildest levels of intervention first. Work your way through all of those before you consider using sprays (after all, almost every spray is going to damage the good guys you're working so hard to recruit as well as the bad guys).

Pest Profile

Flea Beetle

Description: Very small black or brown beetle that leaps (like a flea) when disturbed.

Controls:
- Use a floating row cover.
- Sprinkle wood ashes.
- Cultivate soil (to destroy eggs).
- Plant radishes or bok choy as a trap crop.
- Use garlic spray.
- Sprinkle diatomaceous earth.
- Spray pyrethrum.

And when you do decide to spray, follow the same logic. Start with the least toxic ones first, namely:

Water. Sometimes a good squirting with the hose will wash off aphids or other leaf-clinging critters. Repeat as needed.

B.T. (*Bacillus thuringiensas*). This is everybody's favorite organic pesticide, because it's so specific: it harms only caterpillars. B.T. is a stomach bacteria that kills caterpillars — like those cabbageworms crawling all over your broccoli — who ingest it, but it won't harm worms, honeybees, beneficial wasps, birds, humans, and so on.

Garlic spray. Many a gardener has ground up garlic, made a solution of it, and sprayed it on invaders.

Pest Profile

Japanese Beetle

Description: ½-inch-long oval beetle with metallic blue-green head and copper-colored wings.
Controls:
- Handpick.
- Plant four o'clock flowers to attract and poison them.
- Plant borage as a trap crop.
- Apply milky spore disease to the soil to wipe out the grub stage (over time).
- Cultivate the soil frequently in fall and early spring to expose grubs.
- Spray insecticidal soap.

Horticultural oil. This is the new, improved version of the old "dormant" oil, a product sprayed on pests to smother them when plants were in their off-season, dormant state (otherwise it might smother the plant, as well). The new, ultra-fine grade, of "superior" horticultural oils evaporate more quickly than before, so they can be used all year round, on food as well as ornamental crops. Use them early or late in the day to less likely smother pollinating insects like honeybees, and don't spray on weak plants. You can try to create a homemade oil out of vegetable oil and a little bit of dish detergent (to help the oil stick), but test any such experiments on a small area first, waiting a few days to see if you've damaged the plants.

Soaps. Safer's sells several organic insecticidal soaps, all of which are relatively non-toxic.

Diatomaceous earth. A fine dust, DE scratches insect bodies, causing them to dry out. It works mostly on soft-bodied insects, slugs, and snails. Use insecticidal DE, not swimming-pool filter DE.

Bring Out the Big Guns

These are the heavy hitters in the organic arsenal. They're organic because they're made from natural sources (plants). Their other virtue is that they break down quickly; they don't last long in the environment. But they *are* real pesticides, toxic to insects. Rotenone also poisons birds and fish — and it's not so good for you, either. Wear safety equipment when you use these. Spray or dust only at the end of the day (a still day) so you'll do less damage to pollinators, and clean up properly.

Sabadilla. Cucumber beetles, harlequin bugs, and many other pests on crops like cucurbits, brassicas, potatoes, and beans get knocked out quickly by this fast-acting powder from the sabadilla lily. It breaks down in less than twenty-four hours in sunlight, it isn't too harmful to mammals (although if you're sneezing after using it, you've been overexposed), but it *is* toxic to beneficial bugs, frogs, and fish.

Neem. Made from the tropical neem tree, this extract is toxic only to juvenile insects and takes about a week to work. It doesn't do much harm to adult insects. Neem breaks down quickly in sunlight.

Pyrethrum. This kills a wide range of insects (good and bad), and breaks down quickly in sunlight. Note: **pyrethrum** (or pyrethrin) comes from the painted daisy *(Chrysanthemum coccineum)*. **Pyrethroids** are much more persistent and toxic man-made pesticides.

Rotenone. The biggest organic gun of all, extracted from certain tropical plant roots. It's actually more toxic to humans (and birds and fish) than the common chemical insecticides Seven and malathion, but it does break down much more quickly than those two. It should knock out just about any insect pest you have to deal with (and, of course, all the good-guy bugs that get exposed to it, as well). Definitely the organic insecticide of last resort. (That's why I left it off the list of controls for individual pests — to avoid giving you ideas.)

■ ■ ■ ■ ■

Enough Already

You know, the trouble with talking about insect pests is that eventually it gets kind of depressing. I mean, if all there were to gardening was fighting off six-legged invaders, this endearing hobby wouldn't be a bit endearing.

So let's call it a spray — I mean, a day — and get on to a much cheerier topic . . . like, say, *bird and animal* pests!

13. ANIMAL CONTROL BASICS

FENCE!

14. ANIMAL CONTROL: THE SEQUEL

BURGLAR BREAKS Into Garden!

Well, you have to admit I didn't waste words on that last chapter, did I? It seemed to me that the insect-control chapter went on pretty long, so I thought you'd appreciate a short one. (If you don't like this reasoning, then just consider this book to be like an office building. You know, no thirteenth floor.)

Besides, as this longer treatment of the same topic will amply demonstrate, fencing *is* the first and last word in animal control. I'm not exactly the originator of this thought, by the way: as I pointed out earlier, the word "garden" literally means "walled enclosure."

Is this old definition right? Do gardeners need to be concerned about walling out unwanted creatures?

Consider this scenario. Suppose you went out one morning, sprinkled $20 bills all over your front lawn, then drove off to work. A week later, instead of picking all that money up, you spread out more. Later, even *more*.

I gave a woodchuck an inch, and he took a mile — namely, all my broccoli!

Are you going to tell me that, sooner or later (I'd bet on sooner), that money's not going to sprout legs and *walk* off your property? Of course it is! Well, how can you expect to grow the most lush, succulent, tender crops and flowers you can possibly raise . . . and not have some creatures besides yourself want to enjoy them? It's funny; in the insect chapter, I was telling you the healthiest plants have the best insect resistance. Well, the healthiest plants probably have the *least* animal resistance; after all, since our natural friends have to forage for all their food, they appreciate high-quality vegetation even more than you do.

As Barbara Damrosch put it in her very useful book, *The Garden Primer* (Workman Publishing), "People from the city who move to my area often ask what they can plant to attract wildlife to their yards. 'That's easy,' I tell them. 'Plant lettuce, corn, broccoli, beans, berries, day lilies, yews. . . .' The list is very long."

I like Barbara's answer because it contains both humor . . . and anger. Humor? Well, this is a situation that needs a little humor. Anger? Well, the truth is that nothing, nothing — I mean absolutely nothing — will make a gardener as mad as animal damage to a garden. Insects can be irritating (very irritating), droughts discouraging, and blights blunting, but step outside in the morning and see that — in one night — some groundhog has decapitated every single leaf from every single green bean and you'll be positively *enraged!* Many a peace-loving pacifist has found him- or herself strongly tempted to put shotgun to shoulder after discovering such damage.

Why? Because you feel violated! A cold-hearted burglar has broken into the privacy of your garden, that personal haven of peace and communion, and torn it apart without a second thought. No, an animal raid will get your dander up like very little else.

Inside (somewhere inside), you will know this is a mistake, yes, indeed — a Classic Gardener's Mistake. After all, the varmint that broke in and vanquished your vegetation is fully as "natural" as any swallowtail butterfly or lily you may be *trying* to get in your garden. The creature doesn't deserve such wrath. And you'll know that getting so worked up doesn't do your own self a bit of good, either.

But that inner knowledge won't make you a bit calmer. Animal pests get gardeners' goats, that's all there is to it.

This overreaction is, to my way of thinking, an unavoidable mistake. (Of course, these words do come from a fellow that once *.22-ed a cow* that repeatedly broke into his garden.) And I do encourage you to work on restraining your future response to such occurrences. But I leave that up to you and a highly paid horticultural psychologist. Here we'll focus on minimizing the attacks you do have to deal with.

Animal pests are all the rage.

Fooey to Fences

Now, I don't know about you, but I hate fences. Sure, switchbacking split-rail fences look rustic, and lovely moss-covered stone walls are monuments of beauty, but *they* don't keep anything out. Effective fences, wire or electric, are ugly. They can make a garden feel more like a plant prison than a peaceful retreat.

So I'm going to give you two choices here: you can start out just as I recommended in Chapter 13 — fence your garden right off the bat. If that's your choice, skip over all the succeeding subheads in this chapter till you get to the last one, "The Final Solution."

Or you can try a less preemptive strategy: see how much damage your garden really gets, and what kind of creatures are causing it, and try more moderate measures to handle it. The advantage of this least-intervention-possible approach is economy of both effort and money. After all, it may work; you may not have to fence. The disadvantage is just that: almost every animal-control solution except fencing falls into the "may" category: it *may* work. It has worked for some people, but who knows if you're "some" people or not. It's hit or miss, and when you miss, your garden gets hit. You'll have to accept that.

Some of the measures I'll be suggesting here may sound like "old gardeners' tales." But like the old wives people used to put down (pre-P.C., of course), old gardeners' advice often works. Other times . . . I'll never forget the tale of Marti Roynon, a Chicago gardener who wanted to keep dogs from digging and messing in her urban plot. She heard that lion dung might scare them away, so she dutifully lined a grocery cart with plastic trash bags, pushed it all the way to the city zoo, made friends with the zookeeper, got herself a cartload of fresh "big cat pooh,"

rolled the cart all the way back, and spread the dung all around her little plot.

What happened? As Marti put it, "It just stank so! Worse than the dogs! It was terrible! And you know, the dogs *loved* it."

With that in mind, let's see what we can try that your varmints *won't* love.

Deer

Deer are wonderful, endearing animals that can wreak havoc on a garden. Yep, villains don't get much worse than Bambi. Deer eat

This Is a Vegetable

"I always make gardening mistakes, so many that I've convinced myself that the proper way to learn something is to goof it up.

"One of my favorite mess-ups (to recall) is the time I gave my three-and-a-half-year-old son a full tour through my vegetable garden. As we walked through, I explained to him, 'Now this is a vegetable, you can eat it. This is not a vegetable. This, over here, it's a vegetable. So is this. Not this, though, don't eat that.'

"I came back out to the garden later that afternoon and my son had collected every vegetable in the whole plot! He had cleaned out the entire garden — every baby carrot, every green tomato, the whole thing!

"He had clearly learned his lesson well. So had I!"

— *Larry Hodgson, freelance garden writer in Quebec, Canada, and former editor of both* Houseplant Forum *and* Houseplant Magazine

Deer and tracks

Deer, though beautiful, can be a four-season nuisance in the garden.

greens, scarf down prized ornamentals, and, in winter, fatally chew your trees. And once they've targeted your property, they're very, very hard to deter. Try these control tricks:

- Hang bars of deodorant soap (especially Dial) to repel them. This often works. (Groundhogs, though, love soap.)
- Have an alert dog that sleeps outside.
- Make individual cages out of wooden strips and chicken wire to protect select ornamental plants (such as prized shrubs or emerging tulips) during winter and early spring.
- Spray a solution of one egg in a gallon of water or commercially available deer repellent as needed on vulnerable plants.
- Hang dog or human hair in small cheesecloth or mesh sacks.

- Attach scented dryer sheets to branches. Of course, they look pretty silly, but they *do* work.
- Spread dried blood, blood meal, or fish heads.
- Set up a bright rotating or blinking night light.
- Drape bird netting (it's now actually being *sold* as deer netting) over broad-leafed evergreens and other plantings. Its main advantage is it virtually disappears from sight (very unobtrusive). Its main disadvantage is that when it's hung too low (i.e., ground level) chipmunks get snared in it (*NOT* a pleasant event).

Dogs and Cats

Domestic pets can be both a plus and a minus in the garden. Dogs dig and cats defecate, but both sometimes help keep varmints out of your garden.

Of course, that's *your* pets. *Other people's pets* are almost always a nuisance. If their critters are bothering your cultivars, try these:

- Talk with your neighbors (tactfully) about your problem.

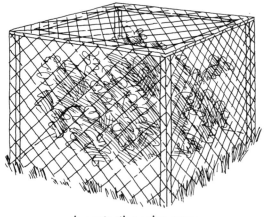

A protective wire cage

- Spray the borders of your plot with a hot pepper solution.
- Grow catnip near the edge of your property to distract feline intruders.
- Don't leave any garbage exposed in your compost piles.
- Have an alert dog of your own that likes to protect its turf.

Gophers and Moles

Actually, moles aren't so bad. After all, they eat insects — including Japanese beetle grubs, wireworms, sow bugs, and more — rather than plants. Yes, their tunnels are unsightly and may provide safe passage for plant-nibbling mice, but try to tolerate moles. Generally, they do more good than harm.

Gophers, though, are a different story. Bigger than moles (12 ounces instead of 3), these fellow burrowers love to chew crop roots and can girdle — and thereby kill — young trees. They also live in groups as big as sixteen or twenty. What to do? Try these:

- Spread human hair, dog hair, ground red pepper, tobacco dust, chili powder, or powdered garlic around the tunnels. Repeat weekly or as needed.
- Stick blackberry or elderberry cuttings in the tunnels — old gardeners' lore.
- Grow castor beans around the garden, or scatter castor bean seeds in tunnels. Mole plant (*Euphorbia lathyris*) is also supposed to be effective. Be careful: both plants are toxic to humans who ingest them.

Moles generally do more good than harm.

Great Thundering Moles!

"Last summer, I hired Windy, a young woman who was totally uninitiated in the art of gardening. As we were planting Sweet Sultan, I fumed about the moles plaguing my garden.

"'Those d___ moles! Look, Windy, step right along this row; can you feel the mole run under your feet?'

"'What?' she exclaimed nervously. 'You can actually feel the moles running?!'

"Imagine — an entire herd of moles thundering through their runs. I don't know who was more incredulous, Windy or I. But I do know that every time I think of that incident, I start laughing all over again!"

— *Ardis Hartwig, who gardens in Los Osos, California*

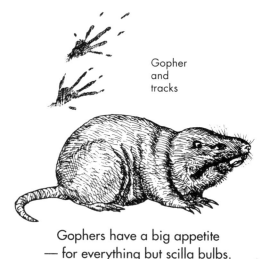

Gopher and tracks

Gophers have a big appetite — for everything but scilla bulbs.

- Spray a castor oil solution (1 tablespoon each of castor oil and liquid dish detergent per 1 gallon of water) on your soil and vulnerable plants.
- Plant scilla bulbs to repel gophers.

Groundhogs (a.k.a. Woodchucks)

How much ground would a groundhog hog if a groundhog could hog ground? Lots, and they do! Mowing and clearcutting are two words I've seen used to describe the near total devastation a groundhog can inflict on your garden. Get a mother woodchuck with her kids, and you're in big-time trouble. They are serious garden predators of corn, grass, peas, beans, broccoli, carrots, and more.

If you're forced to match wits with a woodchuck, try these:

- Trap it. Aside from shooting, it's probably your best bet. A live-animal Havahart trap baited with apples, peanut butter, ripe bananas, carrots, or other goodies will catch most groundhogs. Put the trap in a semiconcealed location near their burrows or trails of matted grass. Release it far away from all other innocent gardeners.

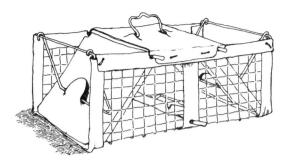

A Havahart trap

- Get a loud dog to chase it off. This probably works best if your dog's bark is worse than its bite. Actual confrontations with wild animals could be harmful to your dog.
- Spread ground red pepper around your garden and its tunnels. Repeat weekly or as needed.
- Remove any woodchuck shelter (brush piles, bushes, tall weeds) near your garden.

Mice

Cute but bothersome, mice will chew potatoes, beets, carrots, crop roots, tree bark (at ground level), strawberries, and many bulbs and perennials. They can cause significant damage. Try these controls:

Groundhog and tracks

Groundhogs are serious garden predators, especially when they bring the whole family.

Mouse and tracks

Mice can nibble everything on the menu from roots to bark.

- Get a cat. This often works well.
- Be careful how you mulch — mulch is a great shelter for mice. Don't put mulch right next to a tree trunk, but leave it a foot from the base. (Also, wrap all young trees with a loose circle of ¼-inch hardware cloth.) In fall, pull your mulch back from perennial and bulb beds until after a few hard frosts. By then the mice will have found other winter homes. (Otherwise your plants may be sheltering *and* feeding them all winter!) And try to use straw, not hay, mulch around your vegetables — mice love the seeds in hay mulch.
- Encourage the presence of snakes and owls in your garden by creating (or leaving) sheltering ground-level and arboreal habitats.
- Scatter fresh or dried mint leaves as a repellent.
- Trap 'em with a mousetrap.

Rabbits

Although Mr. McGregor would disagree, many gardeners don't think Peter Rabbit is as bad a garden raider as his reputation suggests. Most times the critter is too skittish to spend that much time near humans. Still, maybe the rabbits in your area took assertiveness training. In any case, see how much damage they're actually causing before you bother to react strongly to them. Tactics:

- Sprinkle black pepper, ground hot pepper, blood meal, garlic powder, mint leaves, or tobacco dust around your garden. Rabbits always sniff before they eat.
- Spread fox urine (available from hunting or trapping supply stores) around.
- Try the dog-in-the-garden solution.
- Trap and release (elsewhere).
- Wrap young tree trunks loosely with ¼-inch hardware cloth.
- Grow onions, garlic, or aromatic marigolds as a deterrent.

Raccoons and Skunks

Raccoons enjoy melons and other fruit, but their raider reputation is based on one plant: corn. They have a knack for waiting until your

Rabbit and tracks

Rabbits are sometimes blamed for the damage other varmints do.

Raccoon and tracks

Raccoons specialize in harvesting corn at the peak of perfection.

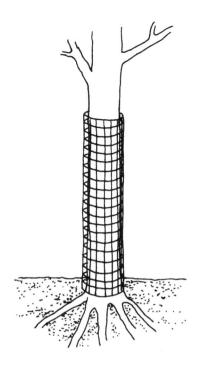

Protect young trees from nibbling rabbits.

sweet corn is just perfect and then harvesting it . . . right before you meant to. And once they discover your corn, they're hard to deter. Better you keep them out *before* they get a taste for it.

Skunks aren't really much of a pest in most gardens. Indeed, they eat a number of harmful insects. But they don't mind snacking on sweet corn themselves. Keep them out the same way you would raccoons. (But if you trap one, cover the cage before you lift it, and move it *very* gently.) Controls:

■ Grow long-vined winter squash, pumpkins, or hairy-stemmed pole beans among your corn to deter 'coons and skunks. Some people swear this works.
■ Leave a radio tuned to an all-night talk station (not music) in your corn patch.
■ Set up a blinking or rotating outdoor light.

■ Cover corn ears with plastic mesh bags, pantyhose, or foil.
■ Trap 'em, beginning *before* your corn is ripe. Peanut butter, sardines, honeyed bread, and marshmallows make good bait.

Birds

Many times, birds can be great for your garden, adding beauty and eating insects. But sometimes our feathered friends do put on bad-guy hats and need discouraging. Most commonly, crows love newly sprouted corn plants, and many species love to raid small tree and vine fruits. When that's so, try these:

■ String fishing line, black thread, or commercially available bird tape near vulnerable crops. These reportedly confuse, and deter, birds.
■ Cover individual bushes or trees with bird netting.
■ Start your corn plants indoors and then transplant them into the garden.
■ Spread lime down corn rows as a deterrent.
■ Try inflatable snakes or owls (they're probably better scarecrows than human figures).
■ Plant mulberries or elderberries near your garden. Birds reputedly like these tart fruits better than your sweet ones.
■ Put red-painted nuts in your strawberry patch before your crop ripens. They may get so discouraged pecking at these they don't come back when the strawberries do get ripe.
■ Cover new corn rows with wire mesh tunnels until the sprouts are a few inches high.

The Final Solution

When your pests flunk the Multiple-Choice Control Test (i.e., they keep choosing "none of

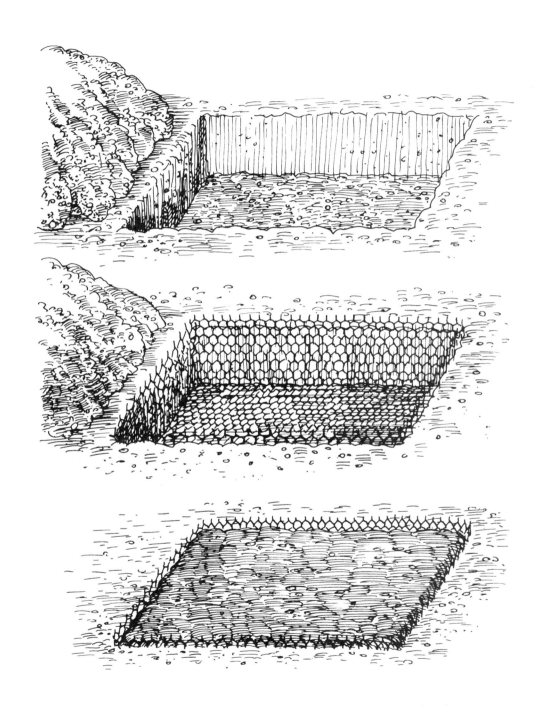

To protect bulbs from burrowing rodents, line the entire bed with chicken wire before filling in with soil and planting.

the above"), it's time to get serious and fence. Fencing to me means just about any wire barrier that protects your plants. Hence, it can vary from a bit of wire screen set over a bulb bed to an 8-foot-high electrified deer fence. Let's start small and work our way up.

Many small plantings can be protected with individual wire cages or barriers. This works above ground, like when you set wire mesh tunnels over corn rows to keep crows from sprouts, and below ground, if, for example, you surround a small bulb bed on all sides with wire mesh to keep burrowing varmints away. (The bulb roots and tops can grow through the mesh.) You can also erect cages for individual prized plants to shelter them during their most vulnerable times. You then dismantle and store the cages, so you don't have to stare permanently at imprisoned plants.

Border Fence

These are all highly effective but small-scale means of defense. A more serious project is erecting a border fence to keep a pest out of your garden altogether. Most times, you'll want to tailor such a barricade to the specific varmint that's giving you trouble.

Burrowing pests. Erect a ¼-inch hardware cloth fence 2 feet below ground and 1 foot above.

Dogs and cats. A 3-foot-high barbed or woven wire fence ought to do the trick . . . or a three-strand electric fence with the strands 6, 16, and 26 inches off the ground.

Rabbits. A wire fence should run a few inches underground and a good 2 feet above, with 2 inch or smaller holes. A two-strand electric fence would have wires 4 inches and 10 inches off the ground.

Under the Spreading Fencepost Tree

"Rather than buy fence posts for our large garden, we cut down some sumac saplings, of which we have an abundance. We removed the limbs and angled the ends so they would go firmly into the soil. They are stable and holding the netting up quite nicely. They are also sprouting new growth, which means they are rooting in our bed. But since everything else (peas, broccoli, brussels sprouts, etc.) is also well established, we can't really pull the saplings out. What seemed like an economical and even attractive alternative was becoming a nightmare.

"Our solution? We pulled two six-inch bands of bark off each of them, and now they are dying."

— *Zoey Haar, one of the newest members of the Storey Publishing family*

Raccoons and skunks. Electric fences work best; run three strands fairly low to the ground. 'Coons can climb most nonelectric fences easily, although some growers report success if the top foot of a chicken wire fence is *un*supported, so it flops back toward the animal when it tries to climb it.

Groundhogs. To be honest, these guys are *hard* to fence out of a garden. You can run a chicken wire fence 1 foot underground and 4 feet above, but don't be surprised if the varmints can get under or over it. It might take 2 feet of underground chicken wire and three strands of above-ground electric fencing to convince Mr. Woodchuck that he'd be better off somewhere else.

Deer. The ultimate fencing challenge — deer can jump a 6-foot fence! Barricading your garden from deer is a major effort. Try attaching bird netting (with twist-ties) to 5-foot stakes. (Netting is now even being sold in 10x60-foot rolls and marketed as deer fencing! What makes it particularly effective, it would seem, is its floppyness — a deer can gauge a rigid fence, but with a moving fence, it can't determine the boundary.)

Serious growers use 8-foot fences . . . 4-foot to 5-foot-tall double fences spaced three feet apart . . . six-strand electric fences running 8, 18, 28, 38, 48, and 58 inches off the ground . . . and truly elaborate (and expensive) commercial set-ups.

By the way, are you a bit nervous about using electric fencing? Well, I don't blame you — they're no fun to touch! But they are actually safe, generally less expensive than wire fencing, and often more effective, to boot. They're also easier to set up than wire fences (no heavy support posts, deep holes, or hard nailing needed) and movable, to boot. They don't cost much to operate, either.

The biggest hassle with electric fencing (once you figure out to turn it off before you touch it — a quickly learned lesson) is keeping the lines clear from grass and weeds. If too much foliage touches the wire, it will short it out and render it ineffective. So you must periodically trim under the wire (turn it off first!) all around the perimeter. On the whole, though, they're a great way to fence.

■ ■ ■ ■ ■

There! Now that you've gotten rid of the insect *and* animal pests, you're ready to enjoy your garden in peace and quiet, right? Well, not *quite*. You see, you've still got to reckon with . . .

AMAZING REMEDIES and Miracle Cures!

Hoo, boy! Have we got a tough topic this chapter! True, there's good news: nearly all plant diseases are plant specific (i.e., they yellow your asters or wilt your cucumbers but don't touch the rest of your flowers or crops). True, as well, the vast majority of your plants will never get struck by disease.

But some will. After all, gardens are right outside, exposed to all the world, and disease can come from the soil, the air, imported plants, insects, even splashing water. You can't quarantine a garden, so you can't keep all diseases away.

And once a disease does strike, it can be danged difficult — sometimes impossible — to deal with. Heck, they can be awfully hard even to identify!

Plant diseases can be awfully hard for garden *writers* to deal with, as well. Dive into the specifics of every single fungus, bacteria, virus, and more that can inflict every single plant and you've got to write a *book* about the topic instead of a *chapter!* No wonder some writers pretty much ignore the subject all together. "Oh, disease?" they may say. "If you raise healthy, wholesome plants" — you know, ones that always brush their teeth and say their prayers — "you'll hardly ever have disease problems. Now, let's get back to talking about seasonal color schemes. . . ."

Loads of Weeds

"I have patrolled my garden seventeen years for weeds — nothing goes to seed here. In fact, one spring when I didn't plant the lower end, the only things that sprouted were volunteer flowers.

"But this past spring, when I learned that some rich black soil across the way was going to be paved under — and realized it could be used to level out an eroded dip in my garden — I got a front-end loader to move it over.

"Now I've got a wide band of foxtail and cocklebur coming up in the middle of my garden. Oh, what did I do?"
— *Jackie Smith, a master gardener in Belle Plains, Minnesota*

"Dear reader, don't ignore plant disease!"

Mind you, I can hardly blame those writers; I'd like to ignore this topic and head straight to Chapter 16 myself. But that would be a big mistake on my part.

Likewise for you, dear reader. The (music swells) Big Mistake with plant diseases is **ignoring them, waiting for them to strike and then reacting.** Let me explain myself by referring to the last chapter. I gave you two choices with animal control, right? Either fence the whole garden right away to secure it, or see what animals invade your garden, how bad their damage is, and if lesser control measures will deal with them.

But suppose you knew that once animals got into your plot, you could *never* get them out — they'd be living *in* your garden for years to come. In that case, everybody would fence right away. The first chapter of every garden book would be "How to Build That Pest-Proof Fence."

Most plant diseases are that hard to get rid of. You can't scare them off with a dog; you can't handpick them; you often can't beat them back with sprays (even chemical ones). I'm not saying that once you get disease in your garden the situation is hopeless. I'm just saying keeping them out is a whole, *whole* lot easier than kicking them out. I'm trying to get you motivated. (Is it hard to get — and keep — yourself worked up about dealing with an enemy so small, you can't even see it? Then just remember: that's one of its biggest strengths.)

For these reasons, I'm going to spend the bulk of this chapter covering the things you can do to help avoid disease problems in your garden. I'll also talk about some basic control measures you can take when you do have problems. (Actually, there's a lot of overlap between those two topics.) But I won't be covering all the particular details of battling black rot on grapes and tobacco mosaic virus on petunias. You'll have to go to plant disease books for those kinds of specifics. Let me recommend two: Barbara Pleasant's *The Gardener's Guide to Plant Diseases* (Storey), an extremely practical, useful, and down-to-earth treatment of this complicated subject, and *Identifying Diseases of Vegetables* (Penn State University), available from many mail-order seed companies.

Prevention Strategies

Keep in mind that, by necessity, I'm speaking in generalities, and they won't all apply to every case. For instance, I suggest keeping plants well spaced to avoid moisture buildup. Well, if tomatoes in your area get leaf diseases, you'd be very smart to do all you can to open up your tomato foliage. But if spinach crops never get sick where you live, you can let their leaves overlap for space-saving and shade-giving reasons and not worry about disease.

Oh, one last thing: what about using chemical fungicides? It's up to you, of course; just remember that most fungicides don't work with just one treatment. They need to be repeated every seven to ten days . . . or each time it rains. Do you want to spend an hour every week getting garbed, applying toxic sprays, then cleaning up the poisons and yourself? Not me, thanks. I'd rather garden.

Strategy #1: Practice Good Sanitation

What was the greatest advance ever made in medical science? It occurred when doctors learned to wash their hands. Sanitation in hospitals has saved more lives than all the antibiotics put together. Go thou, gardener, and do likewise. How?

Clean up dead plant debris. Many diseases overwinter in dead plants, or in the insects that overwinter in dead plants. Eliminate their winter home and you've cut their cycle. They'll have to come into your garden from the outside all over again to get you again.

Burn or hot compost diseased plant debris. If you have plants that were afflicted by disease this year, get them out of the garden — and burn them. You like to recycle organic matter? Put their *ashes* on the garden. You can compost the plants, but only if they all get cooked in a hot compost pile that reaches 130°F. To my mind, burning's more trustworthy.

Don't import diseased plants. Examine every tender transplant or potted shrub you

bring home — carefully — for any sign of disease (mottled leaves, knobby or weak roots, etc.). You might even keep new plants in isolation (quarantined) for a week or two to be sure they're safe before setting them out.

Clean your equipment and trellises. Many diseases can overwinter on your tools or trellises. Use a 10:1 water-to-bleach solution to disinfect them before you store them.

Strategy #2: Use Compost

Compost is *the* elixir, Dr. Grow Good's authentic, multi-vitamin, miracle plant-health restorative. Why? Not just because it helps you raise healthy plants, and healthy plants have better disease resistance (though that's a good reason, for sure). Compost also contains numerous good-guy bacteria and fungi that *fight* disease-causing organisms. Applying compost on a regular basis is as close as you get to inoculating your plants from disease.

Strategy #3: Keep Foliage Dry

Many plant diseases are spread by water; soilborne diseases, in particular, often get to the leaves they infest by splashing up from below. This is why people who garden in dry areas generally have far fewer disease problems than those in damper climes. (I'll never forget the dryland California rose grower who casually said to me, "Black spot? We get a little of that in April, but by summer it's all gone away." Arrghh!)

Obviously, you can't stop Ol' Man Weather from putting your area in damp spells. But if you live in a humid area, you've got to do what you can.

Don't water at the end of the day. Water early so the foliage can dry off.

Better yet, drip irrigate. That way, you never wet the foliage.

Never work plants that are wet. This is the gardener's equivalent of a doctor with unwashed hands going from patient to patient. If one plant you touch has disease, you'll likely spread it to others you touch.

Keep plants well-spaced. If your plants are crowded (by weeds or each other), their leaves will take longer to dry after rain. You'll be creating miniature fog pockets, potential incubators for disease. Likewise, if you can prune plants to give them better air flow and sunshine, you'll reduce their chances of getting sick. This works especially well for moldy ailments like mildew.

Mulch. A good layer of organic matter helps keep plants from becoming water-stressed, thereby contributing to their overall vigor. It also reduces splash, so soilborne diseases have a harder time getting up to leaves.

Make sure your garden has good drainage. If the subsoil stays wet when it gets wet, you have a much greater incidence of rot and other diseases. Check (i.e., dig) to make sure your subsoil doesn't stay waterlogged. If it does, fix it (I told you how way back in Chapter 1).

Roof 'em. This is the radical antimoisture solution: put your susceptible plants under cover. Two years ago, here in western North Carolina, the rains and blight were so bad, not a single organic grower harvested ripe tomatoes — except for those cautious cultivators who kept their plants completely out of the rain. An organic farmer I know who grows his tomatoes in tunnel greenhouses got a good crop. Myself, I had one of my twenty plants survive: the one I'd grown in a barrel under my home's overhanging roof. In extreme situations, you might want to go to such extremes yourself.

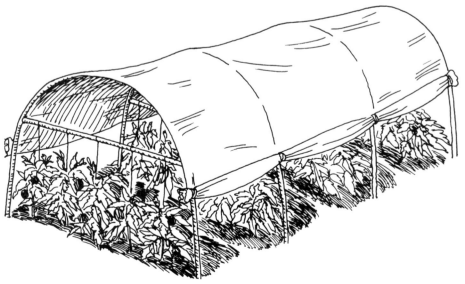

Sometimes roofing plants may be the best solution.

Strategy #4: Rotate Crops

We covered this before, back in Chapter 8, basically for its soil-building qualities. Rotating crops is a great way to break the cycle in soilborne diseases, as well. If scab breaks out on your cucumbers, don't grow cukes or any of its kin (melons, pumpkins, and squash) in that spot for at least one year. Refer back to Chapter 8 for the six family groups you should rotate.

Strategy #5: Grow Resistant Varieties

Plant breeders are constantly working on improving disease resistance of commonly stricken crops and flowers. It's an ongoing process. Breeders come up with a tomato that resists the common strain of early blight; growers use it with success; the blight evolves a new strain that overcomes the resistance; the breeders come up with a newer tomato that resists the newer strain.

You can keep up with the currently most successful cultivars of the plants you grow by paying close attention to seed catalogs. They use key words like "immune," "resistant," "tolerant," or "susceptible" to describe (in descending order) degrees of disease resistance, or code letters like F (resists fusarium wilt), V (resists verticillium), or N (resists nematodes), all of which are explained in the catalogs.

Strategy #6: Time Your Plantings

Like insect pests, some ailments have a peak season. Nematodes (underground root ruiners) tend to build up toward the end of summer, while wet spring weather fosters diseases like bean rust. If a specific disease strikes your area at a specific time, try to plant around it.

Strategy #7: Cover

This advice is for bacteria and viruses carried by insects, such as cucumber bacterial wilt, bean mosaic virus, and aster yellows. Most of these diseases are darned nigh incurable, so you need to keep the bug that transmits the disease from ever biting the plants. However, most of the vector insects are small guys — whiteflies,

Just Trying to Be Helpful

"I still remember my first really big gardening mistake. To learn more about perennials, I started working on weekends for a woman who ran a small nursery. She was an expert gardener, very good at growing hellebores and such, and was quite particular. You had to pick out the plants you wanted and then come back later for them: she wouldn't dig in front of a customer, but had her people box them up and put them in flats.

"One Saturday I was helping out when a woman drove up and opened up her car. I carried out her flat of plants, and then she had me carry out another. And another. And another. Before long, I had filled her entire back seat and trunk. She drove off in a rush.

"Soon the owner came up and saw all the flats that were gone: 'Have all these people been here already?' That woman had driven off with all the orders of the day — over $300 worth of plants!

"And I, young innocent, had carried them all out to her car!"
— *Tim Morehouse, garden columnist for the* Cincinnati Inquirer *and author of* Gardening Basics

DISEASES

aphids, thrips, and mites — and hard to control by ordinary means (including chemical pesticides). Your best bet is to cover susceptible crops with a floating row cover, securing all the edges with boards or soil.

Control Strategies

OK, you've been a good scout; you did all you could to prevent disease but got some anyway. Let's look at the counter strategies we can take.

Cut your losses. Clip off infected leaves and stems to try to keep disease from spreading. When you do, dip your cutting tool in a solution of bleach and water after each incision to keep from spreading the problem instead of limiting it.

Likewise, if it's obvious that a whole plant is going to go down, go ahead and clear it out — it helps to spread more disease as long as it remains — then burn or hot compost it.

Spray with compost tea. I told you that compost has beneficial organisms that can sometimes outwrestle the bad ones. Well, those good little microbes can be even more effective if applied directly — that is, *sprayed* — on the tops and bottoms of afflicted foliage. This technique can also work as a disease preventative.

To make compost tea, mix some compost that has animal manure in it with water and set it in a shady spot to age for two weeks. (The solution'll work better if it's been aged a little; I guess you could say plants like their form of cider "hard.") Strain the odoriferous brew through cheesecloth, add some water if it seems too thick, load up your sprayer or watering can, and thoroughly wet both tops and bottoms of leaves.

As with any fungicide — natural or chemical — you'll need to repeat the treatment every 10 to 14 days to have lasting effects.

Spray with baking soda. It sounds almost too good to be true, but a plain old baking soda solution (1 teaspoon of soda per quart; you might add a few drops of dishwashing liquid to help it stick) can control and prevent mildews and several other fungi on plants. It can even help with some blights. Of course, you'll have to spray regularly.

Spray or dust with sulphur, copper, lime, or Bordeaux mix (a combination of all three). We're pulling out the big organic fungicide guns here. These guys do kill fungi, even in leaves, but they aren't too good for beneficial insects or, for that matter, you. Wear protective clothing when you use them and clean up afterward. Also, spray early, not in the heat of the day, and follow container instructions exactly. Otherwise, you may injure the leaves you're trying to save. (Bordeaux mix, by the way, will temporarily stain leaves blue. It was originally used to stain — and thereby deter — grape thieves.)

Sterilize the soil. If your seedlings tend to get damping off (a mold that topples new sprouts) or plants you pot up frequently get diseased, you need to sterilize your potting soil. Fill a very old pan with damp soil, cover it tightly with tin foil, and stick it in a 250°F oven for an hour. (Warning: foul smell alert! Open windows!) Or you can cook it outdoors for a week or more in the sun by putting it in black plastic bags or covered black plastic pots, as long as the insides heat up to 130°F in the day.

What if a whole area of your garden seems

Need to sterilize? Solarize!

so full of disease that you wish you could sterilize *it?* Don't fumigate it, *solarize* it. This is a pretty extreme measure — it will kill all soil life, good as well as bad, in the top four inches of your soil — but it's pretty effective, as well.

To solarize, or sun-clean, part of your garden, pick an area you can cover with one continuous piece of clear plastic. Then in mid- to late summer when the days are as hot as they're going to get, till (or dig) and fertilize and shape the area as if you were getting ready to plant. Dampen the area well, and then cover it with your sheet of plastic, burying the edges to make a tight seal. Now wait 4 or 5 weeks. The area should heat up so much that the plastic actually swells.

When the time's up, uncover and plant (don't till again or else any disease organisms farther down in the soil may get mixed in near the surface).

That about sums it up for dealing with diseases in the garden. Remember, if "fence" is the key word for dealing with animal pests, "defense" is the word for disease. The more you can do to head off disease problems before they can get there, the happier your plants — and you — will be.

GARDENER TALKS
to His Plants! They
(in Their Own Way, That Is)
Answer!

Puttering — it's such an unassuming, friendly little word. But I do believe it's what separates the men from the boys, the women from the girls, the do-ers from the don't-ers, the green thumbs from the all-thumbs, the — all right, all right, I'll stop. Wait, just one more: the growers from the groaners. Some people basically leave plants lying around in their yard like children's toys they forgot to pick up; others can't wait to get home from work to check on their "little darlings," to see how they're doing and if the poor things are lonely for attention.

I didn't give my tomatoes TLC — and now they're not giving me BLT's!

Think of someone who loves to spend every moment tinkering with engines or someone who really enjoys cooking (I, by the way, am neither of these people) or a child who just won't stop juggling a soccer ball. People who feel that way about gardening, who, like dedicated parents, have high expectations for their plants and want to do everything in their power to help them meet them — these are the gardeners whose plots and yards others will come to admire. They will *observe* their plants, *listen* to their plants, pay one-to-one *attention* to their plants, and *respond* to their plants.

If you are new to gardening, I want to offer you my congratulations. I'm really glad you're giving it a try. I hope you find learning to relate to plants — those vital fellow earthlings who don't talk, walk, or eat out of pet bowls — as satisfying and personally rewarding as so many of us do. I also hope you'll give gardening a real chance to grow on you. Try it for at least two turns round the seasons and see if you catch the (beneficial, of course) bug.

But if after a couple of years, after experiencing the cycle of growth, death, and renewal a round or two from a plant's perspective, after getting over the beginner's stumbling mess ups and moving on to more sophisticated ones — if, after all that, you find you really don't *enjoy* puttering with plants, you know what I say? Give it up. Put your plants up for adoption. There's no moral failure here. Your columbines won't grow up to be concubines; you won't produce delinquents instead of delphiniums.

Indeed, I'd say the classic mistake of this chapter would be to continue to garden if it's not any fun. Find something else to do. We'll absolve you. Heck, we'll even give you your money back for this book. *[EDITOR'S NOTE: ahem — Pat's just kidding in that last sentence!]*

Now what's all this heartfelt counsel (sponsored by your local chapter of Non-Gardeners Anonymous) got to do with this chapter? Simple. This is the chapter on the little things you can do to help your garden really thrive. Heck, weeding *is* work. Fighting pests is no fun for anyone. But puttering around in the plot, doing a little of this and a little of that, is meant to be enjoyable as well as useful. It's the ways we gardeners dote on our plants. It's the extra, caring touches that make the difference between an OK, functional garden and a homey, really loved one.

Let me start with one of the first "extra touches" you'll need to get around to. . . .

Providing a Support System

I — gulp — never supported my plants. My garden's a flop!

Here we're talking not about counseling or finances, but about structures. Lots of garden plants need some physical support, either to get them off the ground or to keep them off the ground when storms and high winds come. Plant supports save space, reduce rot and disease (through improved air circulation and reduced soil splash), and make harvesting much easier.

The key, of course, is to set up your supports before the plants need them — ideally, the moment you put your transplants or seed in the soil. The mistake, conversely, is to put the job off until "later." That's because if you're like me, "later" really means "too late," when the plants have grown so large and dishevelled that trying to erect a support does as much harm as good. Somehow it's hard to motivate oneself to put up a solid support fence for peas when your just-sown seed hasn't even had a chance to sprout. But somehow not putting up the fence right then always ends up meaning not putting it up until "whoops!" time.

Falling in Love

"Here's just a *tiny* sampling of my garden mistakes. I remember, the first time I grew carrots, falling in love with the look and feel of carrot foliage — so much so that I never was willing to thin the seedlings. The result? I got *lots* of lovely fernlets, but no carrots.

"Not one to learn (readily) from experience, I did the same thing with spinach: I fell in love with those lovely little leaves in my new spinach bed and never thinned it any. The result: lots of lovely little spinach leaves, but never any good, eating-size ones.

"And, oh, speaking of spinach, I remember the time I waited until *after* a heavy rain to harvest a big spinach crop. It took three rounds through my washing machine's spin cycle before I got all the mud and grit washed off those leaves!"

— Joy Jackson Kneale, who gardens in Burnsville, North Carolina

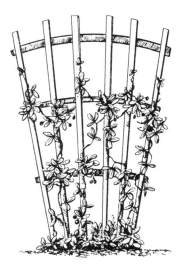

A trellis can be fancy . . .

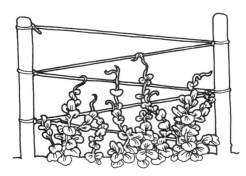

. . . or it can be hand-made.

There are all kinds of supports, some better for certain plants than others. Pictured are a few examples.

Chicken wire on posts. Set 6-foot posts in the ground about eight feet apart and tie 4-foot-wide chicken wire to them. Commonly used for peas.

String and posts. Same post setup, only this time run strong line between them at top and bottom and weave string in a zigzag pattern up and down the length: a classic pole bean support. Some people use a similar setup for tomatoes, with one vertical string per plant.

Brush. Stick wide-branching pieces of brush in the ground and let your plants grow up and through them. Often used for viney flowers like sweet peas and morning glories.

String and stake corral. Set up a hexagon of stakes (bamboo works great) around a cluster of tall, clumpy flowers like veronica. Then run a couple of rings of twine around the perimeter of your stakes.

Single stakes. Drive long, stout poles in the ground next to tall, single plants like tomatoes, delphiniums, or hollyhocks. Tie the plants loosely to the stakes as they grow with figure-eight-shaped loops.

Trellis or arbor. Erect lattice wood (those crisscrossed strips people use to cover home foundations) or attractive entranceway arbors for plants to twine up and over.

Wire cages. Set up a loop of large mesh woven wire around a young tomato plant. (You'll need to tie the loop to some ground stakes or it will blow over, taking the tomato with it.) Your tomato will branch out into the holes and support itself as it grows up. This is easier than tying and retying a growing tomato vine to a stake and more productive, as well, since you don't need to prune off side shoots.

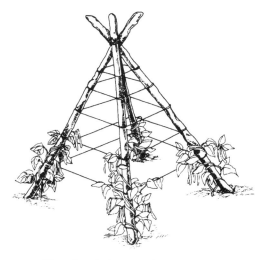

The classic beanpole teepee

Picking, Thinning, Pinching, and Deadheading

I couldn't bring myself to thin those darling little zinnia seedlings. My reward? The little darlings stayed little!

I spent a whole chapter not long ago on weeding unwanted plants. Well, strange as it may sound, you also have to weed *wanted* plants. First off, you'll probably need to *thin* some of them. (If you sow a bed of lettuce or spinach, for instance, the seedlings will probably start crowding each other.) Pull out some of the starts or else none of them will ever grow to full size.

Carrots provide a common example. It's oh-so-tempting to leave all those little green fronds that sprout — why, just think of how many carrots you'll have! The only problem is there won't be a one of them over three inches long because their shoulders rubbed so much, they didn't have enough room to grow. You have to steel yourself, grit your teeth, and thin your carrot plants to a spacious 2 inches apart if you want to harvest roots worth the bother.

The first year in our new garden I started too many tomato plants from seed. I planted them much too close and never thinned them. By mid-summer I had a massive tangle of stringy plants. Two years later, I'm still getting rogue tomatoes showing up among my beds.

There are other types of "good-plant weeding" besides thinning. You see, most plants are, well, lazy: they want to get their jobs over with — to bloom, set seed, and retire (read "expire"). You, on the other hand, want them to keep producing flowers and food as long as possible. So you can't let them finish their jobs. When your blooms set seed or crops mature, the plants get the message that they've finished their work and stop producing.

With vegetables, that means you have to **harvest regularly,** even if you're not going to eat the pickings, and **harvest many crops** — like beans and okra — **small.** Barbara Damrosch (*The Garden Primer*) says that when it comes to vegetable raising, picking is "the second most important maintenance task" right after weeding. I say it *is* weeding — tasty weeding.

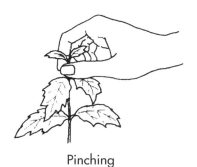

Pinching

With flowers, you can encourage many plants to keep bearing blooms if you cut off all blossoms that are starting to wilt (be sure to get any round ovaries right behind the flowers). This practice is called **deadheading.** If you keep on top of it and regularly remove all spent blooms, deadheading can extend the blooming season of many flowers.

Pinching is another way to encourage a longer flower season. If you clip off the main bud on each flower stalk before it has a chance to develop, the plant will most often produce side shoots that will bloom later (albeit probably a bit smaller). You can pinch (or even shear) part of a patch of flowers and not the rest, so that one section will bloom earlier and the other later. Chrysanthemums, marigolds, and snapdragons are examples of some commonly pinched plants.

In-Season Fertilizing

Some gardeners swear by in-season fertilizing, giving their plants one or two extra bursts a year of nutrition. Others, like me, have sworn it off — partly because we think if you've created good, healthy soil, you don't need to bother and partly (at least in my case) because we don't *want* to bother.

Let me urge you *not* to listen to either the profertilizers like them or the nonfertilizers like me, because either party is likely to be spouting personal opinions or making statements that may not apply to *your* garden. Find out for yourself. Pick a crop or flower. Fertilize half of those plants during the growing season, don't fertilize the other half, and see if it makes any difference. Let your plants tell you if they want the extra nutrition or not. (They may *already* be telling you. If older leaves on plants are yellowing, that may be a sign of nitrogen deficiency. If your fruit crops don't fruit, they may be short on phosphorus. And if your root crops don't root much, they may be short on potassium.)

The Bare Truth

"I wouldn't say this stands as a *mistake*, per se, but it sure does qualify as a confession! I live at the end of a dead-end three-mile dirt road. It's very, very rural. It's gotten a little busier over the years, but back when I'm talking about, sometimes I wouldn't see a car come down that road for a week. When one did come, I could hear it a mile away.

"Well, as isolated as I was, I got into the habit of doing most of my gardening in the summertime without clothes. It's a very relaxing and natural way to garden, really. Only one day, somehow I looked up and there was a giant old Oldsmobile in my drive. I hadn't heard it, the dogs hadn't barked, but there it was — and me without a stitch on!

"It was two older ladies. One got out of the car to talk to me. She sort of looked away while she talked, kind of over my head. I hid behind the tomatoes as best I could, while she talked and talked and talked. (I had been able to grab a T-shirt that was out in the garden, but it didn't exactly come down far enough.)

"Finally, though, I got kind of angry at the whole situation. After all, it was *my* garden. So I just walked out from the tomatoes and talked to her. She didn't act a bit perturbed — just finished up her business and left!"

— *Jim Long, owner of Long Creek Herbs in Oak Grove, Arkansas*

If you do decide to fertilize, the best times are during transplanting, flowering, and fruiting — when your plants are most likely to need some extra nutrient energy. Just work a little extra fertilizer into the topsoil next to your plants (some people call this sidedressing the plants). However, don't overfertilize: supplying too much nitrogen to the soil can promote leaf and not fruit or flower growth.

Should you apply chemical or natural fertilizers? I don't see that putting a spoonful of 10-10-10 next to the roots of your peppers is quite the same as spraying all living greenery with a high-powered 2,4-D herbicide . . . or as building your entire garden's fertility on the big three (N-P-K) chemical powders. So if you want to sprinkle some chemical sidedressing around your plants, go ahead — I won't tell. On the other hand, those of us who prefer natural gardening will in this, as in other things, do things the natural way.

Lots of organic choices are available, including kelp sprays, organic powders, compost (of course), and "garden teas." The last is, in horticultural terms, not a social affair, but a homemade brew made by steeping the ingredient of choice in water, and then applying that to your plants to give them a quick, nutrient boost.

Compost and manure teas are the two most common. As mentioned in Chapter 15, these general garden tonics are easy to make. Fill a big trash can or 55-gallon drum with water, dump in 3 or 4 shovelfuls of compost or manure, and cover. (You can, of course, make smaller batches if you like.) You could stir the brew once a day to help oxygen get in, but otherwise let it steep for 2 or 3 weeks until it's aged some. Then pour it around the base of your plants.

Does a batch of fermented compost or manure do wonders for your garden? Try it and you'll find out. Does it have a bit of, uh, aroma? That, I confess, you won't wonder about for long.

Succession Planting

I missed out on the sweetest harvest season of all — fall.

You may have noticed by now that I'm the type of perfect, on-top-of-everything gardener you should, worshipfully, be modeling yourself after. (I can hear my six-year-old now: "Yeah, right.") Anyway, here's a mistake that, to one degree or other, I still make every summer: I don't plant for fall in summer.

The garden year doesn't end on Labor Day (unless you live in Nome). Many crops can finish growing after the first frost and give you bountiful, frost-sweetened, bug-free harvests . . . *if* you think ahead and plant them back in the summer. Spinach, broccoli, carrots, kale, peas, bush beans, parsnips, radishes, turnips, and lettuce are just some examples.

Actually, I do always plant for fall; I just never do it completely right, because with at least one of the crops, I fail to follow the two crucial rules:

1. **Plant early enough.**
2. **Make sure the seeds stay moist.**

Let's say a crop takes three months to mature and you've got an average fall frost date of October 15. Back up three months from that day and you've got to sow seeds in the middle of July — maybe even a tad earlier because plant growth does slow down in fall. And it's not easy to think about sticking carrot or broccoli seeds in the ground during those busy and hot days of mid-July.

But if you do, come the slower days of fall, when there's naturally less to do and harvest,

PUTTERING

123

you'll be quite glad you did. If you don't, you'll regret it.

Since summer does tend to be hot and dry, it can be hard to keep seeds moist enough to germinate. Or the ground can be moist when you first stick them in but dries out and kills your sprouts before they've gotten big enough to withstand a little dryness. So you must make extra efforts to keep summer-sown seeds constantly moist. Water them at least once a day. I'll often cover them with sheets or even plywood boards to keep the moisture in, checking under the covers every day and removing them the instant crop seedlings start to poke through the earth.

■ ■ ■ ■ ■

Enoch's Walk

The whole point of this chapter is to encourage you to spend time with and pay attention to your plants. As the oft-quoted Chinese proverb puts it, "The best fertilizer is the gardener's footsteps." I can't say it any better than that.

One gardener I know, though, gave me another way of describing the same. His grandfather was so attached to his garden that every evening he'd go for a stroll in it just to visit and check on his fine fronded friends. Granddad was a churchgoing gentlemen, so somehow the two interests got combined in this family and the man's evening stroll became known as Enoch's Walk. (Enoch was a Hebrew in the Old Testament who was described as "walking with God." Indeed, he was so close to God the scripture doesn't say that he ever literally died. He just, apparently, "walked with God" . . . right up off the earth.) This image of an older man on such a peaceful stroll in his garden, on his own "Enoch's Walk," has stuck with me as a model to emulate. Perhaps it will, as well, with you.

17. BULBS, SHRUBS, AND TREES

TREE TAKES OVER YARD!
Bark Worse Than Bite, Says Owner

The cycle of the seasons turns — inexorably, poignantly, yet deliciously. (We gardeners can wax pretty thick about the seasons, you know.) As fall steps front and center, summer chores like weeding, harvesting, and watering begin to drop behind. And your attention should begin refocusing from this year . . . to the next.

Yes, a true gardener's work is never done; it just temporarily downshifts to a lower gear. Autumn is more than the time to finish and tidy up the work of this year. It's also the time to begin laying, piece by piece, the foundations of next.

In other (less precious) prose, fall's the perfect time to put bulbs, shrubs, and trees in the ground — plants that will provide color and grace in your garden for years in the future. Many garden plants do their best when planted in fall. They begin establishing their roots in their new home, sleep through their necessary dormant cycle, and are all rarin' to go when the new spring hits.

Try not to miss this window of planting opportunity. Even if you're not ready to commit yourself to such long-term landscaping decisions as shrubs and trees, you really should stick some flowering bulbs in the ground. It's just too easy and too rewarding to pass up. Watch — I'll show you.

Bulbs

Here — at long last — is (practically) the foolproof type of plant. Bulbs are flowers in a box, complete with their own food supply. Put them under in fall, forget about them in winter, and — surprise! — watch them pop up in spring.

My bulbs never grew (because I never planted them).

Bulbs are so easy to grow that when I asked Sally Ferguson of the Netherlands Bulb Center what is the Number One Mistake people make with bulbs, she said, "Not sticking them in the ground." I nodded sagely — but not smugly. At that very moment I had more than 60 crocus, hyacinth, and daffodil bulbs getting one day closer to spending winter in my mudroom.

125

Sally went on: "Sometimes people buy them but then never get around to planting them. People call me up in March and say, 'I forgot to plant my bulbs last fall. Can I stick them in now?' But by then they're probably dirt balls. Bulbs are living, dormant plants; if you leave them on a shelf all winter, they'll die. So break through your frozen yard with a pickax if you must to get them in the ground, but *do* get them in the ground."

That sounds simple enough, don't you agree?

Particulars

First, the word. "Bulb," in gardening lingo, generally refers to any plant that stores food energy underground. (Some of these are technically corms, tubers, or rhizomes.) Some bulbs are summer flowering, and several of the summer bloomers — like dahlias, gladioli, and tuberous begonias — are frost-tender plants that need to be dug up and stored indoors overwinter in most areas of the country. (Conversely, if you live in an area so warm you do *not* need to dig up tender summer bulbs, you probably *will* have to dig up and refrigerate your *spring* bulbs to give them their required dormant period.)

Let's keep things simple here and focus on the classic early-flowering bulbs, those hardy harbingers of spring that can tough out winter in the ground. Crocus, snowdrop, hyacinth, daffodil, jonquil, anemone, tulip, glory-of-the-snow — there's a whole slew of such colorful plants, short and tall, all eager to grow in your garden.

I'm not going to run through the choices; there're scads of books, catalogs, and garden centers to help you with that. The only purchasing advice I'll give you is steer clear of clearouts. Undersized bulbs give undersized blooms. And damaged or moldy bulbs will likely give you no bloom at all.

Ready to grow? Good. Choose a sunny spot (it can be under a deciduous tree, since that won't produce much shade until after the bulbs have pretty well done their thing). You can prepare a whole bed for bulbs by digging or tilling, or you can just make individual holes with a spade, sturdy trowel, or bulb planter (a handheld tool that cuts cylinders in the earth). You can amend the soil with some compost or organic matter if you feel it's particularly heavy or poor. Likewise, many gardeners put a little commercial bulb fertilizer (which is high in phosphorus) or bone meal (ditto) to give the underground rounds an extra boost.

Stick your bulbs in their holes, about 4–5 inches deep for small ones and 6–8 inches deep for large ones (that depth should include the thickness of any mulch you may put on the surface). Cover them up, adding some of that ever-wonderful soil covering, mulch, if you desire. (Mulch is definitely a good idea where very cold winters might cause the bulbs to "heave" up out of the soil.) Be sure to water them in well — they are living plants so they must have moisture to survive and grow. And if your area freezes hard in winter, that moisture you give them at planting time may be the only moisture they get all winter.

Let's cover some other basic bulb-growing blunders:

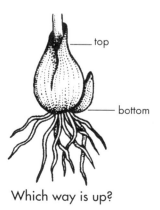

Which way is up?

Putting them in a soggy spot. This is, sadly, a mistake your bulbs absolutely won't forgive. They will, instead, rot and die — every time. "Bulbs don't like wet feet," the Dutch insist. And the Dutch don't kid about bulbs.

Planting them upside down. Your bulbs may well forgive this mistake, but it'll take the tops a lot more work to get up to the top and the roots more work to get down to the bottom. How do you know which way is up? The pointy end (the plant's shoot) goes up, and the hairy end (the plant's root) goes down. If you really can't tell, why, then, plant it sideways. That's much easier for the plant to deal with than being upside down.

Cutting the plants back right after they bloom. A lot of bulbs have some pretty tattered post-bloom foliage. Leave it be; those ratty-looking leaves gather up the energy the bulbs must store for next year's growth. After the tops have begun to brown, then you can cut them down or mow the area if you like. This generally takes about six weeks. Surround the bulbs with other annual or perennial flowers if you want to hide those past-peak bulb leaves.

Leaving bulb debris on the surface after you plant. Chipmunks, squirrels, and mice love to eat many types of bulbs. Why risk tipping them off to your bulbs' whereabouts by leaving pieces of flaked-off bulb skin at your planting spot? (If critters become a real nuisance, you may need to cage your bulb beds as described in Chapter 14.)

Worrying if they start to sprout during an unseasonal warm spell. Don't; they'll be OK. Really. As the ever-helpful Dutch say, "Cold won't nip bulbs."

Barberry's Revenge

"I most regret the day I surrounded my perennial cottage garden with a barberry hedge. Not only was it a prickly terror to prune, it out-competed my flowers for nutrients and light. Last fall, I finally hired a neighbor to chainsaw the hedge to the ground and replace it with a nonspreading split-rail fence. But now I've got 10,000 little barberry plants germinating from seed, when I never had a single berry sprout before. That hedge must have put out a 'Help! I've been murdered!' root exudate."

— Susan Ervin, former
New Alchemy Institute staffer
who tends a beautiful cottage garden
in Franklin, North Carolina

That's about it. Given half a chance, many bulbs will **naturalize** (that is, make themselves at home and spread). If, over the years, they're looking too crowded and producing smaller blooms, you can dig them up after foliage dieback and spread them more thinly. You can also deadhead daffodil, tulip, and hyacinth blooms if you want to encourage them to put energy into roots instead of seeds. (Don't deadhead small bulbs like snowdrop, grape hyacinth, or scilla. Leave them be so they can self-sow and give you more flowers.)

About the only other "mistake" (if you can call it that) you can make with bulbs is to plant too few. They look so great in masses and so lonely when by themselves that more is merrier. You'll probably be more prone to frugality the first fall you plant bulbs. Then, long after you've forgotten all about them, af-

BULBS, SHRUBS, & TREES

127

ter you've trudged your way through an interminably long winter, when yet one more gray-sky day has you feeling the cold weather will never end, when you're trying to decide which is worse, rock salt or mud holes . . . suddenly, bright, cheerful little plants will begin to poke up blooms in your yard. The sheer delight those delicate signs of spring bring will ensure that you'll never plant too few bulbs again.

Trees and Shrubs

While I lustily urge you to stick some bulbs — any bulbs — in the ground in fall, I recommend taking a much more cautious approach when it comes to trees and shrubs. If it's "Go, Go, Go" with bulbs, it's "Slow, Slow, Slow" with the big guys.

Why? Trees and shrubs *are* big. Not only that, most of them get bigger . . . and bigger . . . and bigger. They are permanent landscape elements. (At least, you *want* them to be permanent.) They're not cheap, either. So you want to take your time choosing what trees and shrubs to plant on your property.

Thinking Ahead

My locust went loco, my ash was too rash, and my yew — man, it grew!

I'll leave the aesthetic decisions to you (again, there are worlds of resources for that) and deal here with practical ones. What is the Biggest Mistake with selecting trees and shrubs? It is, of course, the *bigness* mistake — **not taking into account how *big* trees and shrubs will get.** Those puny little sticks you can pick up, pot and all, at the nursery can end up being over 100 feet tall and 60 feet across. Yes, they'll take years to get there (and the waiting part can get frustrating), but unless

you constantly fight to keep them from reaching their natural size, in time they will. It's a pain in the pruners to have to cut back a foundation bush or driveway tree every single year to keep it from taking over — why add an extra chore to your life when you can, with just a little forethought, avoid it? Plus, if you have to clip or shear plants every year, they never develop their pleasing, natural shapes, but are stuck with the visually artificial ones you impose.

And things can get worse. That yew or maple you planted so close to the house can become an actual threat to it. The roots or limbs can create so much damage, you'll have to remove the whole plant and end up, many years later, right back where you started.

So, please, be sure to give them the elbow room they'll need to grow. One gardener recommends deciding what trees and shrubs you want at an arboretum — where you'll (Army recruitment music, please) see all that they can be — rather than at a nursery.

Giving a Plant What It Needs

I put a peach tree in a frost pocket. It was the pits!

Well, if too big a plant is Potential Problem #1, the opposite — too little a plant — is #2. What I mean by this is that **if you put a tree or shrub in an inappropriate location, it may never reach its healthy, natural size.** (It may even die.) "Location, location, location!" is the cry of the forlorn tree or shrub, not just the storefront business owner. So if your new landscape plant doesn't like wet, don't give it wet. If it's unhappy with dry, just say no to dry. Give sun lovers sun, shade lovers shade.

Most importantly, speaking of location, don't plant something that's inappropriate for your climate. Your area's too-cold winters or too-hot summers will do a plant in — if not in the first year then the second year or the third year — *some* year. (Instead, consider using some choice "native" plant — one that's indigenous to your area.)

I hope it doesn't sound as if I'm making too much of a stink about all this. Actually, growing trees and shrubs is easy. They're nonfussy plants that basically take care of themselves — *when* you take the sensible precaution of putting the right one in the right spot. So do plan for these plants. It's worth it.

Planting Time

If you live in a temperate nonfreezing climate, you can plant virtually any tree or shrub in fall. That will give their roots plenty of time to get used to their new home and do some initial growing before the high-demand spring and summer growing season begins.

If you live in an area with hard freezes, the best general rule I've found is that fall is a good time for planting deciduous (leaf-shedding) plants, but not so good for evergreen ones. Evergreens, particularly broad-leaved (as opposed to needled) ones, may dry out during winter because moisture gets sucked out of their foliage on sunny winter days, moisture that new transplants can't replace from frozen ground.

So plant your evergreens in early, early spring, when they'll have at least some chance to do as much settling in as possible before the real growing season commences. (You can plant deciduous trees and shrubs then, as well, if you wish.)

Tree-Planting Myths

All right, let's dig some dirt. Due to recent research into what happens with different techniques, a couple of the age-old rules for planting trees and shrubs have been changed. Some concepts that were commandments just a few years ago are considered Basic Mistakes today. To wit:

Tree/Shrub-Planting Myth #1: Don't put a $5.00 plant in a 50¢ hole. This old, perfectly

Too Close Is Too Bad

"Overplanting trees and shrubs — it's easy to do. I live on a normal-sized city lot, about 60 feet by 120 feet. When we first moved in, it was just a few trees and junipers and the typical infinite lawn. After I tore out the trees and lawns, there was very little left. It looked all bare.

"Well, I saw all that bareness and what could I do? I overplanted like crazy. And, already after just three years, I can see that some of those shrubs and trees are going to have to go. The purple-leaved smoke tree is getting too close to a hemlock. The big yellow tree peonies go so well together with that witch hazel — they're both a lovely shade of pale yellow — but they're getting *too* together. The peonies are going to get shaded out by the witch hazel.

"I'm going to have to move a lot of big plants around and into the backyard to get it all straightened out. I should have planted perennial or annual flowers in some of those gaps instead of packing the spaces with trees and shrubs. Flowers are a lot easier to move around."

— *Jan Whitner, Seattle gardener and the author of* Stonescaping

BULBS, SHRUBS, & TREES

129

sensible-sounding idea led many gardeners to put goo-gobs of soil amendments and fertilizers in their planting holes. More recent research, however, indicates that making a planting hole too attractive can entice the roots to stay in those rich, cozy confines, as if they were growing in a container, rather than spreading out the way they should.

This doesn't mean you shouldn't make *any* effort to improve the soil in your planting holes. If, for instance, you're planting in heavy clay, lightening up the soil with some organic matter can be helpful. Just don't get carried away with planting-hole enrichment.

Tree/Shrub-Planting Myth #2: Dig deep so the roots can easily grow deep. It turns out that tree and shrub roots spread *out* more than they spread down. The old idea that a tree's roots look like an upside-down, mirror image of the tree's top has not held up. Many trees and shrubs don't have deep taproots at all. Instead, their horizontal (lateral) roots a few inches below the soil surface spread out twice or three times as far as their branches.

So make your planting hole as *wide* as possible, not as deep as possible. The more of the soil around the root ball you can loosen up, the better.

This all goes to show that you and I aren't the only gardeners who mess up: even experts can make mistakes with their expert advice! Isn't that consoling?

Dig In!

Dig that hole, as I said, as wide around as you have the energy for. But try not to make it a single inch too deep. Why? The big goal here is to have the plant growing at the exact same height it was before you got it. (You should be able to see a soil line on the trunk if you look closely. Incidentally, some trees also have a

rough wooden "ring," a graft line, where one type of top was joined to another type of base. Make sure any graft lines stay above the soil.) If the tree ends up sitting a little high, that won't do any harm, but you definitely don't want it ending up too low. That's another reason for not digging deep: if you dig or loosen any soil under your planting hole, it may settle a bit after you put the plant in, and some of the tree's trunk may end up buried.

How do you make sure your hole isn't too deep? You can measure the hole's depth and the root's depth (lay your spade across the hole to see where the soil line of your hole is). Or, if your plant isn't too heavy, check

Too Much, Too Dry, Too Close

"Six or eight years ago, we put in a few clumps of Chinese bamboo, *Phyllostachys* species, that we got from Georgia. It's now covering half an acre and spreading. It's grown fifty feet tall, where it was only supposed to reach ten, and has started to supplant the neighboring oak-hickory forest. We're worried that it actually may take over Casey County. Take it from us, don't fool with bamboo!

"Want more? I once planted some trees where I couldn't get water to them. When a dry spell came along, they just gave up. But that wasn't as dumb as the time I planted some trees under a power line. They did fine; that is, until the power company came along to clear their right-of-way."

— *Greg Williams, editor of* HortIdeas, *a fine monthly newsletter on current horticultural research*

by just putting it in the hole occasionally as you dig.

Next, with a garden fork, loosen the soil around the sides (not the bottom, remember) of your planting hole to encourage root spread. You can even poke the tines into the soil out beyond that to aerate the roots' future happy hunting — uh, growing — grounds.

What you do next depends on whether your tree or shrub is **containerized, balled-and-burlapped,** or **bareroot.** If it's containerized (grown in some kind of pot), the job's a cinch. Get the plant out of the container by holding the container upside down and knocking on its bottom or, if necessary, by cutting off the container. Try to disturb the roots as little as possible in this process. Put the plant in the hole (at the right depth, of course), loosening up any roots that may have started to circle around in the container.

If it's balled-and-burlapped (wrapped and tied in a burlap or plastic sack), set the plant in the hole and cut off the wrapping so it can't possibly restrict roots' growth. It's harder not to disturb the roots this time, but do the best you can.

If it's bareroot (surrounded by no soil at all), you need to build a cone-shaped mound of soil to spread out the roots on, making sure, as always, that the plant gets set to the right height.

Finishing the Job

OK, the plant's in place. Begin filling the hole, packing the dirt snugly around the roots to eliminate air pockets. When the hole's about two-thirds full, flood it with water. Soak it really well. That will help pack the soil and also get rid of air pockets. Then finish filling the hole, and give it a final, deep watering.

Now if you've planted a bareroot tree, examine its branches: have some of them been cut back? If so, great; you're done. If not, get some pruners and cut off ⅓ of the wood of the tree (including some of its top). Why such drastic pruning? Because the roots of a bareroot

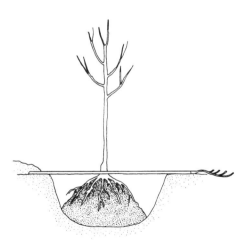

Lay a long-handled tool across the hole to make sure the mound is the proper height.

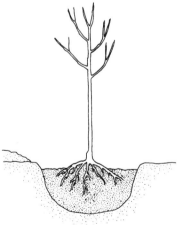

When the hole is about two-thirds full, soak it with water.

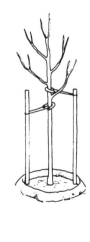

Staking a tree is optional.

plant have generally suffered so much in re-moval and transport that they can no longer support the foliage they did before. Cut back some top growth to compensate and the tree should recover just fine.

Some other common suggestions:

Should you build a little moat of soil around the planting hole? Sure, if you want. It may help a little more water get to the roots during those early haven't-grown-out-much weeks.

Should you stake the tree to provide support? That's OK, if you're really concerned about harsh winds. Tie the plant to the stakes loosely so you don't risk cutting into its trunk — and remove the stakes after a year.

Should you whitewash or wrap the trunk to prevent winter sunscald? That won't hurt and certainly may help. Such splitting in the bark can occur on sunny winter days, particularly on fruit trees in northern climates. A spray of thinned white latex paint will eliminate the possibility.

Should you loosely encircle the trunk with woven wire to keep rodents or rabbits away? Yes, definitely. Otherwise, they may nibble the bark around the trunk and kill it.

Should you mulch around the trunk? Absolutely! You know why? To keep you (or who-ever) from mowing or string-trimming into the trunk! **The number one tree-and-shrub pest is . . . guess who? You and me: human beings!** One of our power tools gets a little out of control and — slice! — yon tree is felled or irremediably gashed.

A collar of 3–4-inch deep mulch is the ab-solute best defense against this. So yes, spread a wide ring of mulch around the base of the trunk. The mulch shouldn't touch the trunk, however, or it can encourage rot or nibbling rodents.

Of course, wonder garden elixir that it is, mulch serves other beneficial functions. It helps stabilize the ground temperature, reduc-ing the chances that your plant's roots will

The real worst pests of trees and shrubs

frost-heave right up out of the ground during that first winter. It conserves soil moisture. It cuts down on grass competition (after all, trees and shrubs don't have to compete with grass in the woods).

Over the life of the tree, however, mulch won't really make a big difference in the moisture or competition departments unless you spread it way out beyond the drip line (the outer rim) of the tree or shrub. After all, as you recall, roots roam out quite far. But that's all right. That little ring-around-the-tree mulch will still keep those deadly mowers and trimmers away.

Ongoing Maintenance

Once your plant's snugly tucked in and protected, can you forget about it?

Pretty much. Oh, you can fertilize it once a year if you like. Just be sure to spread that fertilizer out away from the base, out where the feeder roots grow. You can prune it occasionally, a topic so big that I'll (gulp!) have to tackle it in a later chapter. And you can sit back and enjoy it all the time.

One thing, though, and one thing only you must *not* forget to do, Best Beloved: water. All during its first year of growth, any time your area hits even a bit of a dry spell, give the ground around your tree or shrub a deep, thorough soaking. It is all too easy to neglect this. The vegetables, the flowers — it's obvious those little frail things will starve for water. But sturdy trees and shrubs, you scoff? Give me a break!

I killed my sapling by ignoring its need for water!

Indeed, they will. You'll be able to snap off all the dead-and-dry branches you want if you don't water your young trees and shrubs. Plants this big, they may not show their water stress until it's too late. And *especially* during that first year, the roots of that new little tree or shrub have not spread out far and wide enough to weather dry weather.

I walk with a limp on this one, friends. My favorite tree of trees is the American beech. And I killed the first one I ever planted . . . by neglect. To make my sad story short: "July. Hot. No water. No tree."

Mind you, it's a very good idea to water, deep and slow, around your trees and shrubs during *any* extended growing-season dry spell. But during that first year, it's not just a good idea — it's a *life-saving* one.

NAKED TREES KILLED by Winter Wind!
Chilling Sight, Say Police

I tell you, sometimes I'm afraid I'm turning into the Nagging Nabob of Plant Care. All the time I'm telling you, "Do this, don't do that." Did you have an overprotective parent? "Dear, put on your mittens — it's supposed to get down to 65° today." "You better not go down that slide, Sweetie. It doesn't have seat belts."

Am I starting to sound like *that?*!

Have we gotten to the point where you picture me as an over-picky, finger-pointing fuss-budget who glares over your shoulder every time you go out to garden? If so, sorry — it can't be helped. After all, it's my job to give you a whole bookful of advice, with special emphasis on the "don't do's" side of it. (And remember, I *am* an expert on things you're not supposed to do.)

I bring up this concern now because, if there's ever a chapter that could make me sound like a picky perfectionist, this is it. Every fall, all garden writers crank out a high-handed column on all the things you ought to do to get ready for winter. It's officially required. We gather in the Journalist Team Huddle come August and our coach — uh, editor — says, "All right, gang, it's Autumn. So let's *ought 'em*. Get out there and pile on that fall gardening guilt!"

Well, I've had it. I'm breaking ranks. I hereby say, "Aw, who cares? Don't do *any* of this stuff if you don't want to."

Why such daring horticultural heresy? Has

Auntie Pat is after you!

Stone gone off his wheelbarrow? Is he a few tomatoes shy of a vine?

No, indeed (not any more than normally, anyway). My point is simply this: **while all the advice I'm about to give you is sound and reasonable, almost none of it is absolutely essential.** Skipping most of these suggestions will not kill your plants (heck, it's fall, most of 'em are about to die, anyway).

True, the tips I'll share are useful. They can give you crops earlier next year than you'd ever have thought possible. They can take care of some chores during a fairly slow garden time that you'll otherwise have to tackle during those hectic weeks of early spring. They may improve your soil's fertility or help head off next year's insect, disease, or weed control problems. They are good things to do, and I recommend getting around to as many as feels reasonable.

But it's not a crisis if you don't.

So you want to know the **Classic Mistake of Winter Preparation**? Guess what. **There isn't one.** Garden life will still go on, whether you do most of these steps poorly or omit them altogether.

The Ten Commandments — uh, Suggestions — of Fall

There! Don't you feel better? Guilt-free gardening, that's my new motto! Now you can look over the following ten steps as suggestions — not commandments — choose the ones you want to do, and enjoy the doing of them. *Enjoy!* After all, that's what gardening is all about.

1. Clean Up

It's the oldest advice in the (garden) book: **clean up all the dead plant debris from this**

year before the garden starts resting up for next. This advice has two strong points: it removes the diseases and the pests that overwinter in plant litter. That's two good reasons. Of course, a picked-up garden looks neater, as well. Other than that, though, why bother?

2. Cultivate or Cover Crop

If your vegetable garden has a lot of soil pests or the soil in it is fairly chunky, you may want to **till or dig it up in the fall.** That way, birds and cold weather will have all winter to kill exposed pests, and the alternate freeze-thaw cycles will help break up tough soil clods.

On the other hand, if your soil's in fairly healthy shape, it's better to **leave it with plant cover** so it will suffer less erosion over winter. Better yet, **plant an overwintering cover crop** (a topic we covered way back in Chapter 5) like winter rye mixed with hairy vetch. That way you'll not only protect the soil, you'll also build its fertility at the same time.

Winter cover crops are a great way to do some good for your garden when everyone else's is just sitting there.

3. Test the Soil

Fall is the best time to test your soil. For one thing, the testing services are less busy then. And for another, the amendments you add (based on your test results) will have more time to break down and work their way into the soil than if you add them in spring. (For the how-to of soil testing, turn back to Chapter 5.)

4. Protect Tender Crops

Most areas experience an early frost or two, then enjoy an "Indian summer" warm spell before winter comes in for good. If you **protect tender plants against those early hits of cold,** you may get a few weeks of good growing out of them. Baskets, buckets, blankets, straw, plastic sheets held off the plants by hoops . . . there are a lot of things you can use to provide short-term shelter. Such improvised protectors won't work every time, but it sure is rewarding when they do.

5. Sow Spring Greens

Back in the "Puttering" chapter (No. 16), I talked about planting crops in summer to enjoy come fall. Well, in many areas of the country, you can **plant crops in fall that you'll be able to harvest next spring!** It is truly rewarding to have a leaf crop spring up in spring the way those flowering bulbs do. It gives you a chance to enjoy greens weeks, even months, earlier than you would otherwise.

Pick hardy leaf crops like lettuce (Winter Density, Oak Leaf, Boston, and Black-Seeded Simpson are hardy varieties), spinach, corn salad (also called mâche), and winter cress. Sow them a couple of weeks before the date of your average first fall frost (ask a fellow gardener or county extension agent for the date). Protect them a little, if you want, with one of those floating row covers or a little straw mulch. (In one test, lettuce under a floating row cover survived -5°F!) Then forget about them until spring. Simple as that.

6. Plant Garlic

Garlic may not bloom the way daffodils do, but it is another bulb that (in most sections of the country) does best when planted in fall. Garlic puts on its biggest growth during the longest days of the year — in June — so the bulbs that end up the biggest have already done as much growing as possible before then. Ergo, **fall-planted garlic cloves get bigger than spring-planted ones.**

Poke your cloves (note: that's cloves, not entire heads), pointy end up, in well-prepared soil, about 1 inch down and 3 inches apart. Then mulch them right away with a light covering of leaves and a couple of inches of straw. Don't skip this step: mulching will help protect the bed from winter frost heaving and — even more important — spare you *hours* of tedious weeding around tiny garlic stalks next spring.

7. Put Away Your Tools

In my case, that first means, "Find your tools." It's amazing how weeds love to hide hoes (I can't imagine why!). Anyway, it doesn't do your trowel or hose or spade or tiller or plant

Overwinter Woes

"I run a small native plants nursery, but I don't overwinter my plants in a greenhouse. I just let them endure the winter outdoors. I may lose 10 percent of my stock overwinter that way, but it's cheaper than building and operating a greenhouse.

"Three years ago, I decided to try to offer the plants a bit more winter shelter. So I stacked thirty or forty flats, six to eight deep, right beside my house. I had about twenty species: jack-in-the-pulpit, wild geraniums, green and gold, sweet woodruff, foamflower, coreopsis — some nice plants.

"Unfortunately, when the water drained off my roof, it fell right on the flats and rotted almost all the plants. They — and I — were decimated. And, of course, the plants I left out like I had before came through the winter just fine!"
— Craig Mailloux, owner of
The Elk Mountain Nursery in Asheville,
North Carolina

WE'D LOVE YOUR GOOFS!

We hope you enjoy this book. If you have some gardening goofs of your own, we'd love to have you share them with us so that we might help other gardeners avoid making the same mistakes. (Plus, it's fun to read about gardening goofs!) Thanks for sharing. *Pamela B. Art*

Publisher

My biggest gardening goof was _____

_____

_____

Comments about this book: _____

_____

_____

☐ You have my permission to use my comments in ads, brochures, mail, and other promotions used to market your books.

I purchased *Real Gardeners' True Confessions* from _____

☐ Please send the latest Storey's Books for Country Living catalog.
☐ Please send information about Pat Stone's quarterly magazine *GreenPrints*, "The Weeder's Digest," the only magazine that shares the human, not the how-to, side of gardening.

Name: _____
Address: _____
Signed: _____ Date: _____

From: _____

BUSINESS REPLY MAIL
FIRST-CLASS MAIL   PERMIT NO.2   POWNAL, VT

POSTAGE WILL BE PAID BY ADDRESSEE

STOREY'S BOOKS FOR COUNTRY LIVING
STOREY COMMUNICATIONS INC
DEPT TC
RR1 BOX 105
POWNAL VT 05261-9988

Coddle your tools.

fencing a whit of good to spend winter out-doors. **Round 'em up and bring 'em in.**

Hand tools will appreciate it (you can tell 'cause they'll purr quietly) if you scrape off any dirt, and rub them down — both handles and blades — with vegetable oil to prevent metal rust and wood cracks. Motorized tools will be more likely to start next spring if you drain or run their gas tank dry (otherwise, the fuel may, over time, absorb water) and discon-nect the spark plug.

8. Take In Tender Plants

Houseplants that you've let take the air all summer, tender perennial bulbs (like dahlias), frost-sensitive herbs (like rosemary and sage), and any other plant that doesn't like cold but may survive if reared in the cozy indoors for a few months . . . well, they won't get the chance if you don't **bring them in before the first frost hits.** Right? Right.

9. Mulch and Water

I really shouldn't have to tell you this one; after all, we covered it just last chapter. But, just in case . . . don't forget to **mulch and thoroughly water newly planted bulbs, shrubs, and trees.** If the fall weather is dry, water *all* your shrubs and trees hard. They need that water round their roots going into winter, because once the ground freezes up (assuming you live where such gosh-awful things happen), they won't be getting any more water until spring.

I started this chapter by saying most of the suggestions I'd be giving are optional. This one isn't — not if you want to be sure these plants live.

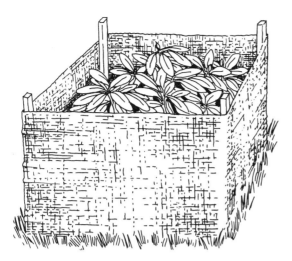

Give tender shrubs and trees a break
— a windbreak.

10. Protect Vulnerable Shrubs and Trees

Do you live where the winter winds are harsh? Where the sun and cold can virtually assault innocent little shrubs and trees? If so, let me make one last suggestion, one for new or particularly exposed plantings.

Protect them. Wind, sun, and cold can dry out such vulnerable plantings, even if you did water them in fall. So consider putting up a snow fence in front of a new hedge or putting in four stakes around that tender young shrub and wrapping burlap or snow fence around those posts. This will also help protect them from nibbling deer. Use some material that slows the wind but doesn't completely block it (for example, not plastic). Total wind barriers cut off air circulation and may create seasonally unhealthy heat buildup.

■ ■ ■ ■ ■

There you have it: Stone's Ten Fall Suggestions. They're not hard. They're not all absolutely necessary. Basically, they're good ideas for fall. Really, winter preparation is pretty much a relaxing, easy-to-understand topic.

Not at all like the one that's coming on the very next page.

The Cold Truth

"We live up in the northern part of Vermont, near the Canadian line. Not surprisingly, our biggest early mistake was trying to grow things that just don't survive -40°F winters. Apricots, grapes, cherries, forsythia, and some roses — most gardeners can grow them, but we just can't. Our subsoil is limestone, so — again, we had to learn the hard way — we can't raise acid-loving plants like blueberries and azaleas unless we grow them in pots.

"We love to mulch, but the cold quickly taught us a lesson about that. When we mulched crops like bush beans late in the season, they froze quicker than if we'd left them unmulched, because the mulch kept soil heat from protecting the plants."

— *Lewis Hill of Greensboro, Vermont, author of a number of fine gardening books, including the classic* Pruning Simplified

HEMLOCK ATTACKED with Shears:
For Its Own Good, Gardener Claims

Part of the reason I wrote this book is to help people get over being *intimidated* by gardening. Too many times, I think, people let feelings of nervousness or inadequacy stop them from getting out there and playing with plants. To that I say, "Don't fret. After all, if you accidentally pull up all your zinnia or carrot seedlings this year, you can always plant them again next year."

I'm so intimidated by pruning that I NEVER attempt it!

But *pruning* — even I admit being intimidated by pruning. First of all, I don't really want to do it. I mean, why go hacking away at some innocent, dormant plant? Isn't that unfair or something? Shouldn't I just let it grow the way nature intended?

Besides, pruning sounds complicated. I mean, there are sizable books devoted exclusively to the topic. (One of them, Lewis Hill's *Pruning Simplified,* is extremely helpful, by

the way.) Worst of all, I'm afraid of making some dumb mistake that's going to ruin the plant forever. I mean, it's one thing to let a batch of lettuce seedlings dry out. It's quite another to butcher those prize azaleas that grace the front yard!

The Cunning Cutter

I'm confessing to all these fears in case you feel them, too. Obviously, I don't blame you if you have such feelings, but I want to urge you not to let them hold you back — and not just because a basic knowledge of pruning is a very important plant-care skill. It turns out that pruning is a fascinating process. Through it you'll learn a lot more about how your plants work and grow and, as a result, become closer to them. Combining botanical theory (how plants grow) with application (taking cuts into your own hands) will increase your appreciation of plants and your own role in their prosperity. The wonderful result is that learning to prune truly helps *you* grow as well as your plants.

139

If you're shy, be bold! If you're bold, be shy!

So if you're the type who tends to be a bit shy about pruning, don't be. Be bold! Gain an understanding of what you're aiming to do, then cut away, my friend, cut away! A general rule in pruning is that **you can cut up to a third of most plants away without harming them.** That's a lot of pruning, shy types!

Conversely, if you're the more aggressive type with a natural tendency to cut, cut, cut to keep things neat and under control, restrain yourself, *mon ami.* First, learn what you're doing. After all, another general rule of pruning is that you should **always have a reason for every cut.** You may be keeping certain plants from thriving — or even blooming at all!

To put the above two thoughts in my ever-popular Classic Mistake terms, the Two Classic Mistakes of pruning are, being shy if you're shy . . . and being bold if you're bold. **Shy people, be bold! Bold people, be shy!** Them's my pruning mottos!

Pruning Principles

What makes pruning complicated — and worthy of entire books on the subject — is the fact that all plants and pruning jobs aren't the same. Different plants have to be pruned differently. You can hack a forsythia to the ground if you want, but you had better barely nip a Scotch pine. You also need to prune differently depending on *why* you're pruning. A line of hemlocks in a hedge need regular spring trimming, but a specimen hemlock standing alone will probably only need to have damaged or unhealthy sections cut out.

Different plants should be pruned at different times, as well. A flowering shrub that blooms on old wood (wood that grew last year) should not be pruned until **after it blooms in spring,** or you'll cut off all of this year's flower buds. A flowering shrub that blooms on new wood (this year's growth) should be trimmed

A Moment of Marital Miscommunication

"Soon after we settled into our home fifteen years ago, I planted the narrow border beside the fence. Back then, it was a sunny strip of ground, its midsection lightly shaded by a small maple. I tucked rhubarb and sweet cicely into the dappled shade, reserving the sunny spaces for daisies and hollyhocks. And at the far end of the border, I strung a trellis and planted sugar snap peas.

"As the years went by, we added more gardens, put on a deck, and built a tiny greenhouse, but this unassuming border remained essentially unchanged. Gradually, though, the daisies began flopping over and the rhubarb turned anemic, while the cicely threatened to completely take over. Compost, fertilizer, and extra water did no good. In one of those "Aha!" moments philosophers live for, I realized the trouble: shade. That friendly maple now stretched higher than the house, throwing deep and unrelenting shadows over the entire flower bed. My semi-sunny border had become a woodland garden.

"Or it needed to. So this spring, I set out to make things right. My husband, a man who doesn't mind digging, pried out the rhubarb for transplanting near the pumpkin patch. 'It needs more sun,' I told him.

"While my patient spouse wheelbarrowed some compost to the border, I lifted a few ferns from behind the garage. 'These can take the shade,' I said. I prattled on about native plants, about adapting to a changing landscape. He dug, turned, lifted, and (I thought) listened. At last we were through, and I drove off to the garden center to check out its current crop of ferns and forest dwellers.

"When I returned I found him on tiptoes atop the picnic table, holding the long-handled loppers high above his head. At his feet were maple branches. Lots of them. The border was basking in more sunshine than it had seen in a decade.

"'The badminton birdie kept getting caught in the tree,' he explained. 'I thought I'd just take out some of these twigs.'

"And then the kicker: 'You said this was too shady, right?'"

— Christine Kindl, garden columnist for the Greensburg, Pennsylvania, Tribune-Review

as early as possible in the season, before that new growth has had a chance to grow.

Despite these differences, the basic principles of pruning are widely applicable. Getting them under your belt will help make sense of — and demystify — all the pruning you'll do. Surely the first principle is . . .

Have a Reason

Dead and diseased wood. When a branch snaps off in a storm, it leaves a ragged, open wound that is slow to heal over. If you cut it cleanly back to the trunk, the tree can much more readily seal off that section and protect itself from any invading diseases. Likewise, if a limb has already fallen prey to disease, cutting it off and disposing of it (burying, burning, removing far away) may keep the disease from spreading to the rest of the tree.

Control or shaping of an ornamental. When that lovely lilac off the porch or the yew out front starts to outgrow its space, regular

PRUNING

141

pruning can help keep it in bounds. There's a hitch here, though. If keeping a plant from getting too big becomes a constant battle, it may be time to face reality and get rid of it. Many a homeowner has planted a cute little shrub or tree in a spot where it causes trouble later — when it's not so cute and little anymore. You may be able to keep it in bounds by regular restrictive pruning, but it will be a never-ending responsibility and will probably give your plant an artificial, forced appearance, as well. Much better in such a case to, uh, cut your losses by going to the ultimate pruning — *removal*. Replace it with a specimen whose natural growth habit will fit in the space.

As a general rule, while you can redirect and control the shape of many ornamentals, the more you're inclined to **work with their natural tendencies,** the less pruning work you'll have cut out for you. Still, many plants, even if they don't get too big, may have a natural tendency to get overly dense. An annual thinning to help open up the interior and relieve overcrowding may be just the thing to keep them healthy and attractive.

To increase production. Almost every fruit crop — tree, vine, or cane — needs annual pruning. Unpruned, most of them get overgrown and the result is likely to be small fruits — and fewer and fewer of those. Unpruned, many fruit trees will bear only every other or even every third year instead of annually the way you want.

To make a hedge. Living walls of plants can be great privacy or windbreak screens. But since rows of plants won't naturally grow into a nice, solid barrier, you'll need to give hedges some regular persuading, in the form of pruning. (A hedgerow of mixed plants can be let grow more freely if you have the space and location for a more natural-type barrier.)

There are plenty of other reasons to prune — to prepare a plant for transplanting; to rejuvenate an old worn-out plant into a younger, more productive one; to create a topiary (a plant with a sculptured shape);

My Topiary Magnolia

"About ten years ago, I was a seasonal worker at Brookside Botanic Garden in Wheaton, Maryland. One day we went out to rescue plants from a soon-to-be-razed house; the owner had many nice plants he wanted saved and donated to the Garden.

"While we were working, I found a little Southern Magnolia seedling under a conifer. Nobody else wanted it, so I took it home to grow. Without thinking about it, I stuck it within three feet of the corner of my house, right near a rain gutter.

"Ten years later, that plant is almost 35 feet tall — it sticks out ten feet above my house! I had to prune a lot of the lower branches to keep them from blocking the narrow path beside the house. Then I had to prune even more when I got my house repainted.

"Now the first 10–15 feet of that tree is completely bare and the rest is really narrow. The whole thing looks like some top-heavy topiary! If those Plant Amnesty people — that group that advocates 'tree-friendly' pruning techniques — ever got hold of me, I'm sure they would put me in jail!"

— *David Els is assistant editor of* **The American Gardener** *magazine.*

and so on — but, hey, I am *not* writing a book on the topic. No, it's time to prune away any more talk about principles and move on to techniques.

Pruning Techniques

Basic Technique #1: Cut to a Bud

One pruning technique stands out as the most basic and vital of all, yet I bet most people with clippers haven't really thought about it. So let's take a moment to start . . . where plants start. Does the hair on your head grow from the bottom or the top? The bottom, right? Do the trees in your yard grow from the bottom or the top? (Watch out: this is a trick question!) It must be the top — otherwise, those words that Daniel Boone carved in a beech tree more than 200 years ago — D. BOONE/KILLED BAR/ IN TREE/1760 — would now be about 200 feet off the ground!

Trees and shrubs grow from their tips, or rather, their buds — leaf buds. (Yes, they bloom from buds, too — flower buds). Generally, they extend from the **terminal buds** at the end of twigs. That dominant tip can actually produce hormones to keep the **side buds** from sprouting and creating competition. When you cut off that terminal bud, the side buds then become free to grow, changing the direction of the plant, making it more bushy — whatever you determine. Many plants even have hidden side buds, called **dormant** or **adventitious** (I love that word) **buds,** which will spring into action once a terminal bud's been terminated.

To direct growth when you're pruning, **always cut to a point just above a bud.** Cut too

Cut above a bud and at a slight angle to repel rain.

PRUNING

143

far above a bud and you'll just leave a stub of dead wood on the end of the plant, open for possible disease infection.

Since many times you'll prune to help open up a crowded plant, you'll often want to deliberately cut just above outward-facing buds. That way the new stems that start out from those buds will naturally want to grow out.

Conversely, if you want a tree or shrub to start filling in its middle more (for aesthetic reasons or because, say, you live in a dry climate and need compact plants that use less water), you could prune back to inward-facing buds, so the new branches would start to grow into the middle.

Basic Technique #2: Remove Limbs Properly

Sometimes for health or redirection purposes, you'll need to cut off entire limbs. You always want to **cut these back all the way,** either to the branch they sprang from or to the plant's main trunk.

If it's too big to cut off with a pair of hand clippers or loppers (those clippers with long handles), it's too big to take off with one cut. If you try to, the limb may tear off before you can finish sawing, ripping off some of the bark and wood back in the main trunk. In other

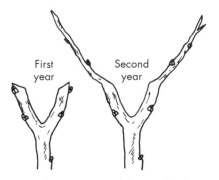

First year   Second year

Prune above outward-facing buds to encourage spreading growth.

words, if you have to *saw*, don't do it in one cut. Do it in three. Here's how.

Basic Technique #3: Health and Safety First

You want to promote tree health, not risk making it worse, so **always use sharp tools** that make neat cuts. And whenever you are pruning for disease control, **dip your cutting tool in a sterilizing bleach-and-water solution** between cuts so that you won't possibly *spread* the disease yourself.

Speaking of health, take care of yours. Don't go climbing around in trees, at least not any higher than you're willing to risk falling (it happens). And definitely, no chainsaws. They're for cutting firewood, not for making clean pruning cuts. And *definitely,* definitely **no chainsaws up in trees.** (Are you crazy or something?!) If you need to make big cuts up in trees, it's time to close this book and hire a tree-care professional.

Pruning Particulars

All right, let's talk about specific plants. I won't cover everything (this is a chapter, not a book, remember?). In fact, I'm going to steer completely clear of roses. There're so many different kinds of roses that, accordingly, need different kinds of pruning, they'd need a chapter of their own.

Still, the guidelines below will help with most of your pruning situations.

Shrubs

Timing. Many shrubs are grown for flowers. But remember that *when* they flower determines when you prune. Shrubs that bloom in spring should not be pruned until after — right after — they bloom. Otherwise, you'll cut off their flower buds. Summer bloomers can be trimmed in the dormant, early spring off-season. They'll then have time to grow new wood for this season's blooms.

Cane shrubs. Ornamental plants, such as forsythia, bamboo, hydrangea, weigela, nandina, Oregon grape, and kerria, are vigorous growers that send up new branches from the ground every year. These guys are tough — you could mow them down to the ground during an off-season pruning and they'd come back to life. So what you're generally trying to do is thin these zesty growers out a bit, cutting any canes you remove all the way back at the base.

1. First, get rid of any dead wood. (Can't tell if a cane or branch is live? Scratch it lightly with your fingernail and see if it's green underneath.)

2. Cut out any canes that cross all the way from one side to the other of the plant.

3. If it's too crowded in the middle, thin that out some.

4. When a plant's too tall, cut out the tallest canes one by one until you have it under control. It's OK if it ends up a bit shorter and smaller than you like. It'll grow, you know.

Mounding shrubs. Small-leaved, thin-stemmed shrubs like barberry, spirea, Japanese holly, abelia, evergreen azalea, and escallonia are easy to keep under control. Just start with the longest branch. Cut it out as far down in the bush as you can reach. Now find the newly anointed tallest branch and cut it out. Repeat until the shrub is a manageable size. This technique will give a shrub that is smaller but still has a natural shape.

Treelike shrubs. Be more careful with shrubs like witch hazel, cotoneaster, rhododendron, camellia, and deciduous azalea — some of these don't like much cutting. Cut out the dead wood and, if you can, leave it at that. If more is needed, take out a few crossing branches and overcrowded ones. But don't cut too much; if a lot of tall, vertical shoots (water sprouts) come up the next year, you've overdone it.

Trees

With all trees, start with the health-promoting basics. Cut out diseased or damaged branches. When two branches are crossing or growing too closely parallel, cut out the smaller one. If a branch hangs down too low (at an angle below horizon-

Dashes indicate where to prune.

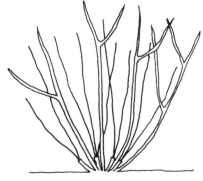

One year after pruning

tal) or leaves the trunk at too narrow an angle (a very narrow V-shaped crotch), it's more likely to break off than ones that come out at more normal angles, so consider trimming them out. Now let's break trees down into various types.

Deciduous ornamentals. If you want to do any shaping of a deciduous tree, do your cutting in the off-season, preferably right before spring. (Cutting frozen wood may not be good for the tree.) The key here is **the younger the tree when you start, the better.** Do you want an open space underneath the canopy? Then when you feel that the upper parts of the tree are large enough to support future growth, cut off a few lower branches at the trunk. Do you want to limit the future height of the tree? Don't wait until it reaches that height and then "top it." That will make the tree look as though it got beheaded. Trim it some as it grows so it will still be in proper proportion when it reaches its final height.

Evergreen ornamentals. *Needle-leaved evergreens* (like pines and hemlocks) are a bit tricky. Unlike deciduous trees that grow all season long, most evergreens put on their year's new growth during a short period in the spring. If your goal is to shape an evergreen into a nice bushy shape, you'll need to do your cutting *during* this growth spurt and you'll want to

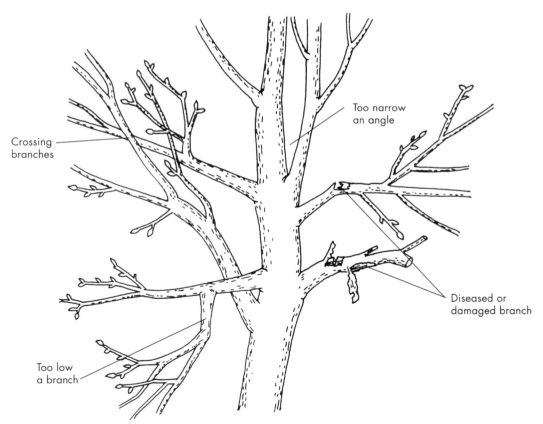

Crossing branches

Too narrow an angle

Diseased or damaged branch

Too low a branch

All trees should get a basic "good health" pruning.

trim the new growth, not the old. (They will not send forth new growth from cut old wood the way many other plants do.)

That means that once your hemlock or yew gets tall, it's very difficult to try to trim it into a bushy shape. You have to start trimming it

Saw off limbs in three steps

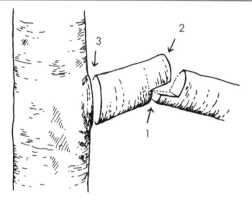

1. A few inches out from where you'll be making your final cut, saw up — less than halfway — into the limb (not any farther or the limb will press down and bind your saw).
2. A bit closer to the trunk, saw down all the way. The limb will then fall without shearing or binding.
3. Make a clean cut all the way down through the limb stub, which isn't heavy enough to rip back into the trunk. Make this cut close to the trunk, but be sure to leave the branch collar, the raised ring of wood where the limb attaches to the trunk. The branch collar contains all the mechanisms and hormones for tree wound self-repair, and works better than any store-bought tree-wound dressing.

into shape by gradually "tightening up" its new growth while it's small, even though that will slow down the tree's overall growth a bit. Get it "in shape" early, then trim it back a bit each year to help it keep that shape.

Broadleaf evergreens, like azalea, mountain laurel, and rhododendron, aren't quite so fussy. To keep their overall growth from getting too loose, **cut off the small terminal buds** of new sprouts — not the fat flower buds — in early summer. If you want to keep the plant from putting energy into producing seeds, **deadhead fading blossoms,** as well.

Hedges. I'm sneaking hedges in here, even though some consist of shrubs, not trees, because you treat them pretty much like bushy evergreens. You're going to **shear them** (cut them back at their tips) **during their most active periods of growth.** With evergreen trees such as hemlocks, that means you should cut during their annual spring growth spurt.

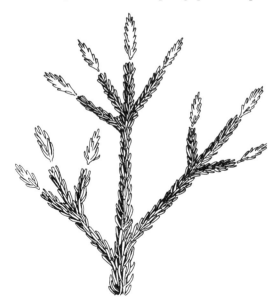

Shape-prune needle evergreens only on their new growth.

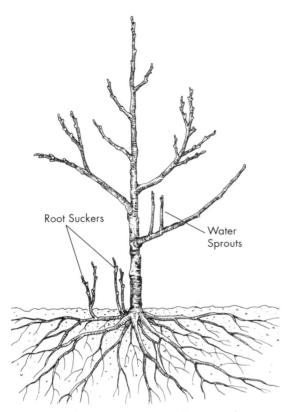

Root Suckers

Water Sprouts

Prune all water sprouts and root suckers.

With all-season-long growers like privet or barberry, you need to shear more often — partly depending on how fast they grow and partly depending on how neat-edged a hedge you want. Basically, if they look to you like they need shearing, then shear them.

Remember to clip the sides as well as the top. And make sure the hedge is wider at the bottom than at the top so the bottom leaves can get enough sunlight to stay healthy.

Fruit trees. Fruit trees need annual pruning to be productive. Otherwise, they'll tend to get too crowded and produce small fruits. Worse, if left alone, many trees only fruit every second or third year. So after performing the necessary health-care steps, make sure the tree isn't overly crowded and that the center of the tree is open enough to receive light and have good air circulation.

The first thinning step will probably be to cut off any **water sprouts** (young unproductive vertical shoots, often caused by previous pruning) and **root suckers** (vertical shoots coming up from the ground).

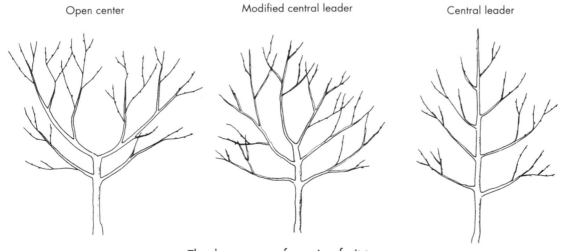

Open center

Modified central leader

Central leader

The three ways of pruning fruit trees

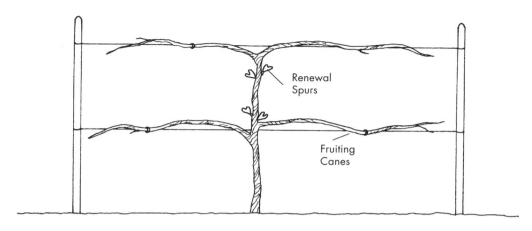

Grapes, the four-arm Kniffen way

After that, thin to relieve overcrowding and to start molding your tree into the shape you want. That will probably be one of three choices: central leader, modified central leader, or open center.

Central leader trees have one main trunk with side branches. **Modified central leader trees** have a main trunk that has been topped to keep it from getting too tall. **Open center trees** have had their main trunk completely cut out so that the side branches dominate and the interior of the tree receives maximum sunlight.

I didn't take my tree to its leader, and now its growth is completely chaotic!

Apples, pears, and cherry trees are generally trained to have central leaders. If that leader starts to get too tall as the tree ages, or to bend back over and shade part of the rest of the tree, most growers cut it back, creating a modified central leader.

Plums, peaches, apricots, and nectarines are generally trained to an open center shape.

Smaller Fruit Plants

Grapes. Grape pruning is not for the squeamish. Older wood on grapes does not bear fruit. Only year-old canes, which are smooth and tan (not dark and ridged), will grow grapes. And most grape vines can support only four of those canes well. Everything else should go.

Most growers use the **four-arm Kniffen system,** training the vines to send out canes onto a higher and lower support wire. To do so, during the late-winter off-season, select four healthy canes, one on each side at the higher wire and one on each side at the lower wire. It's a good idea to tag them with colored ribbon. Then choose four more branches near the first four that you'll cut back to make *next* year's canes, and tag those as well.

OK, (swallow hard, now) cut everything else off. Then cut the future canes, called **renewal spurs,** back to short branches with two or three healthy buds. Now cut this year's canes so they're each about five feet long. Not much left? Don't worry; your grapes will show their appreciation of your courage come harvest time.

PRUNING

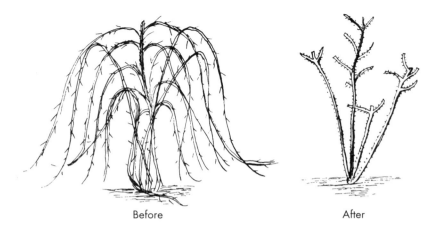

Before   After

Brambles, before and after pruning

Blueberries. Here again, last year's growth is key: those branches will produce this year's fruit. Since that means encouraging new growth *this* year to give you fruit *next* year, the main step to pruning blueberries is **getting rid of the really old wood.** So cut out, all the way down at the base, any wood that's four years old or more.

After that, **thin.** Cut out branches that droop all the way to the ground, any overcrowded branches, and any too spindly branches.

Blackberries and raspberries. Most "bramble" fruits are biennial: the first-year canes produce leaves; the second-year canes bear fruit (and then die). So start pruning them by **cutting out, at ground level, all the canes that bore fruit last year.** Do this during their dormant off-season.

Next, **thin the remaining canes until they are about 6 inches apart.** Reducing overcrowding will lessen disease and increase fruit size. Then cut back the canes that are left to the height of your support wire (generally about 3 feet) so they'll be

less likely to flop over. (You do have a support wire for them, don't you?)

If you're growing everbearing raspberries (those twice-a-year bearers that give a strong early-summer harvest and a weaker fall one), you might try this trick: pick one section or row of your patch, and cut *all* the canes in it clear to the ground. That section won't produce an early-summer harvest at all (because you cut out all those one-year-old canes) but will give you a good-sized harvest in the fall!

■ ■ ■ ■ ■

A Cutter's Credo

There! That's all I'm going to say about pruning. If you're still a bit intimidated by it, even after my remarkably clear and erudite explanations, don't let that stop you. Just prod yourself on with this thought. As my apple-farming neighbor, Jamie Clarke, once told me, there's only one thing worse than pruning your plants. That, of course, is *not* pruning your plants.

20. SEED STARTING: AND SOW ON

HOME GARDENER
Starts Seeds Indoors — Successfully!

I am absolutely delighted that seed starting turned out to be the topic for the last chapter. Logically it fits because, while seed starting is something every gardener should be able to do, it's not easy and really isn't a basic skill that most beginning gardeners are ready to tackle. So it makes good sense to put it at the end of this book.

But the reason I really like ending with this topic is because it's so appropriate. What better way to close the loop of one gardening year than by opening up the loop of the next? Sending you off to your gardening future with a tray of home-nurtured seedlings in your hands is the absolute finest gift I could ever hope to give.

Besides, if there was ever a topic that brings out my expertise at making mistakes, seed starting is certainly it. Indeed, the real garden experts say that every gardener should keep a detailed record book. I don't. If I did and anyone looked into it during the months of February and March, I'm afraid they'd title it *The Confessions of a Serial Seedling Killer.*

In my dreams, I see the courtroom where I'd be put on trial — the jury, a double six-pack of certified Master Gardeners; the prosecutor, the author of *Gardening for the Utterly Perfect* (Whopper Press).

"Isn't it true," Sir Perfect sneers, "that you killed an entire tray of broccoli seedlings by *overfertilizing* them?"

"At least I was trying to feed them," I plead.

"That you permanently stunted more than two dozen foxgloves by starting them in brick-hard garden soil instead of using professionally aerated planting mix?"

"Just once," I say.

"That you actually *roasted* a flat of lettuce starts by leaving them in a *closed* cold frame on a sunny day? That your strawflowers got lean for lack of light? That you didn't base-heat your basil? That, in all, you neglected to follow the seed starter's credo: L.S.M.F.T.?"

"Lucky Strike Means Fine Tobacco?"

"*SILENCE,* you horticultural hoodlum!"

It's true, of course, I have snuffed out some seedlings in my day. But who hasn't? Indoor seed starting is not easy. For one thing, it means learning that, to a seed starter, L.S.M.F.T. stands

151

for Light, Soil, Moisture, Fertilization, and Temperature — and that you have to pay close attention to all five if you want your seedlings to thrive.

But there's more — so much more — to starting seeds than making mistakes. When you turn your breakfast table into a miniature hospital nursery where you sow packets of tiny brown seeds; when you spray and warm and fertilize and provide light, doing your best to turn little question-mark-shaped sprouts into green exclamation points of life; when you even flub up sometimes and have to put some of your offspring *under* the ground instead of into it . . .

When you do all that, that's called *caring*, plain and simple. And that's what it really takes to make a garden — and a gardener — grow.

Why Not Buy Your Seedlings?

I really think the experience of "parenting" a plant from start to finish is the most rewarding reason for starting your own seeds, but, of course, there are practical benefits, as well. After all, if you start your own seeds, you'll have a vastly greater variety of crops, flowers, and herbs to choose from than if you trot down to the local garden center to pick up six-packs of nursery-raised starts. From old-fashioned sweet peas to Dutch cauliflower to bronze fennel, a world of plants will be yours to explore right at home. You'll also be able to time your plantings so the seedlings will be ready to go into the ground at just the right time for your area.

But as I've already said, it ain't easy. I can't pinpoint one Classic Mistake with seed starting . . . because there are so many you can make. And that's because there's so much to deal with. You really do have to pay close attention to five factors — Light, Soil, Moisture, Fertilization, and Temperature.

Just as important, you have to realize that *seeds* and *seedlings* are different things that need to be treated differently. Think of seeds as babies in the womb and seedlings as the newborns in the nursery. Anyone who's been a mother knows there's a world of difference between those two.

Let's begin with those wonderful kernels of potential . . .

Seeds

The first time you open one of those cute little seed envelopes, you wonder if things so small will ever amount to much of anything. But, of course, they will eagerly enact their own version of Jack's beanstalk — if you keep those five words in mind.

Let's take it one word at a time.

Soil

I'm going to start with what I see as most important. To me, the first step is to make sure you have an appropriate growing medium for your plants. Maybe this is because I've so of-

Morning Glory Madness!

"I nicked my morning glory seeds, as instructed, and then put them in the oven on a wet paper towel to germinate more quickly. Needless to say, I forgot them and they 'cooked'!"
— *Meredith Maker, graphic designer at Storey Publishing*

> ## Homemade Planting Mix
>
> - Five parts of leaf mold (or vegetable-based compost; manure composts may contain disease)
> - Four parts good topsoil
> - Two parts sharp sand
>
> Mix together thoroughly.

ten used inappropriate mixes that became adobe-hard after a few waterings.

That's the rub: your mix has to stay **light and friable.** For that reason, *don't* (repeat, *don't*) use plain garden soil. You should be able to find a store-bought planting (not growing) mix locally — or you can make your own using the recipe above.

Some growers start seeds in straight horticultural vermiculite ("popped" mica flakes) or a mixture of vermiculite, milled sphagnum moss, and perlite. Such ingredients are very light and hold moisture well. They have little nutritional value, but seeds contain all of the food they need in order to germinate.

What will you put your planting mixture in? Cut-off milk cartons, deep-sided disposable aluminum pans, special styrofoam seed-starting systems — all will serve. Your containers need at least 3 inches of depth for roots to grow and small holes for drainage so those roots won't rot. Many gardeners prefer to make their own wooden flats (14 inches by 12 inches by 6 inches is a good size). Leave about a ⅛-inch gap between the bottom boards so extra water can drain out, and then cover this base with newspapers or leaves to keep the soil from draining out, as well.

Note: Some gardeners put their plants through two indoor growing stages. They start them in one flat and then **prick them out** to another roomier flat for a few weeks before transplanting into the garden. If you go this route, you might want to make your starter flats longer and shallower, say 14 inches by 23 inches by 3 inches.

Temperature

This is a big one. I can't tell you how many seeds of mine never sprouted because I didn't make things warm enough for them. Most seedlings will germinate better if their soil (not air, mind you, *soil*) temperature is 70°F or above (some germinate best at 90°F!). So **keep your seed trays in a constantly warm place.** *Don't* stick them in a windowsill: it's likely to be too cool.

Probably no other factor will increase germination rate and decrease germination time more than temperature. Indeed, if you want to go to the extra step of buying a bottom-heating seed propagation mat or rigging your own out of garden-center heater cable, you will have *impressive* germination success. I guarantee it.

> ## Warm Places to Start Seeds
>
> - The top of your water heater
> - Over a gas stove's pilot light (caution: some plants, such as tomatoes, are susceptible to gas leaks)
> - Above a floor register
> - Behind a wood stove (but keep them high enough to avoid floor drafts and check often for drying out)
> - Over a fluorescent grow light (they generate some warmth at their ends)
> - Any warm spot you can find

SEED STARTING

153

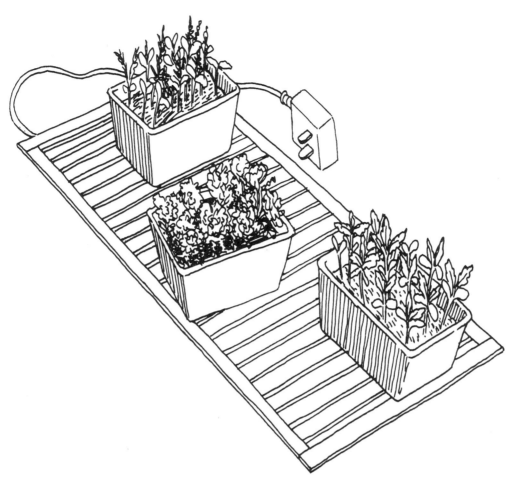

A propagation mat will greatly improve your seed-starting success.

Actually, I had thought about keeping this a secret (gotta save something for the sequel, you know), but heck, I figured I could share it with you. (You won't tell anyone, will you?) A heat mat boosted my seed-starting success so *considerably* that now I never sow indoors without it. A heat mat makes me look as though I know what I'm doing; that's all there is to it.

Moisture

Seeds need to be kept constantly moist in order to germinate. Two key words here: *constantly* and *moist*. Never let that soil dry out.

On the other hand, don't flood it, either. You want the mix moist but not soggy — like a lightly wrung-out sponge, as experienced gardeners always say.

That means **wetting your soil thoroughly before you plant, and not letting it even begin to dry out afterward.** Some people drape a sheet of plastic wrap, polyethylene, or cloth on top of their planted seeds to keep that wetness in. (I do.) Try that if you like, but be absolutely sure to check it every single day to see if any seeds are starting to sprout. If they are, immediately remove the cover so they can get some light. (If you don't . . . well, I *wouldn't* know from experience, of course, but some people tell me the smothered starts will rot right quick.)

Some gardeners moisten their seed containers from below by periodically putting them in a pool of water in the sink. Or they rig up bottom-soaking systems: setting the containers on bricks in water, or running a cloth (diapers work well) from the bottom of a container down to a pool of water. Such set-ups can wick moisture up to the soil above.

Many gardeners, though, simply water — very faithfully — from above. The only hitch here is you can't just douse your unrooted seeds with H_2O or they'll wash all over everywhere. Gentle, gentle! Use a plastic sprayer or a watering can with a fine, upward-pointing rose (the sprinkler head) so the drops will lightly fall on the soil. Failing that, at least drizzle the water through your fingers as it falls, to break it up.

Your water should be at least room-temperature warm. And if chlorinated water comes out of your tap, better let it air a day before using so that that plant toxin will have a chance to evaporate.

Light

Most seeds don't need light to germinate. Think again of a womblike environment: warm, moist, and *dark*.

A number of flowers, though, do need some light to sprout. Columbine, cosmos, godetia, lobelia, mignonette, nicotiana, petunias, stocks, and strawflowers are just a few that need to be planted on the surface of the soil or covered only very lightly. (On the other hand, bachelor's buttons, calendulas, globe amaranth, nasturtiums, pansies, *Phlox drummondii,* most poppies, and sweet peas should be sowed under soil the way vegetable seeds are.)

Fertilizing

Fertilizing is actually *not* necessary — not for seeds. They carry their own food inside their shells.

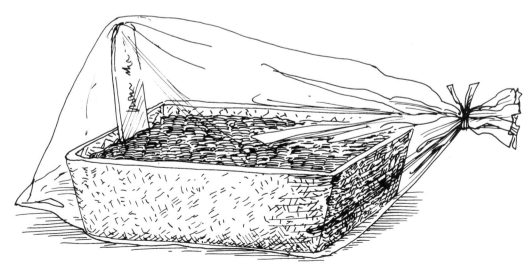

A cover can help keep ungerminated seeds moist.

Labeling

Now that you understand the five basic conditions necessary for germinating seeds, you're ready to plant — or almost. First, you need to assemble a pen with *indelible* ink and some popsicle sticks, strips of stiff plastic, or purchased plant labels on which to write the plant name, variety, and date sowed.

Don't skip this step. Neglect to label your flats and you'll be surprised how quickly you lose track of which seeds are which. (I know. I've done it.)

Timing

One other thing and you'll be ready to sow: timing. Most gardeners time their plantings relative to the average date of the **last spring frost** in their area. (Find that out from neighboring gardeners, a county agricultural extension agent, even the local weatherperson.) Depending on the flower or crop, you might want to plant your seeds anywhere from 4 to 10 weeks before that frost date. The accompanying timing chart will give you approximate sowing and transplanting dates for some common plants.

Ready? Set? Indoor Sow!

Let's grow. Fill your containers almost to their brims with well-moistened soil. Smooth it out. Then begin carefully setting your seeds in. Plant them shallowly — the rule of thumb here is to **set them to a depth just three times their diameter.**

In fact, to keep better track of where you've planted, you may want to set all your seeds on the surface of the flat and then sift extra soil mix on top to cover them. (With flower seeds that need light, simply press them into the surface and cover with a sheet of glass or clear plastic.)

If you're using individual containers, you'll want to put only a couple of seeds (the extra one's for insurance) in each container. With flats, space your seeds a half-inch apart if you intend to transplant them to a second, grow-out flat later, or one to two inches apart if you're going to keep them in the same flat until garden time.

Hot Compost? No, Burning Soil!

"For several years, I've started seeds in a 3x4-foot wood box filled with Pro-Mix planting mixture and heated with a buried soil-heating cable. One night last May, I was closing up the house and smelled something peculiar. I checked the oven and decided that might be it; we'd broiled salmon for dinner. But when I went down to the basement to turn off the lights over the seed box, the smell was much worse. I touched the Pro-Mix — and got a mild shock! When I looked close, I saw smoke coming out of the feverfew seedlings!

"I ended up shoveling all the Pro-Mix into pails, which I took out into the driveway and hosed down. Some of the soil mix was actually live coals. They were still smoldering the next morning!

"Obviously, my heating cable had shorted out, which was due, I think, to the fact that I had removed some transplants without replacing their soil mix, so the seedbed overheated. Would I say the whole experience unnerved me a little bit? Well, I'm buying my plants this year!"

— *Gwen Steege, editorial director at Storey Publishing*

Timing Chart

Here are some sowing and setting-out dates for a few vegetables and flowers that are commonly started indoors. Use them as approximate guides; the best planting times will vary depending on your locale and gardening practices.

Plant	Sowing Date (weeks before last frost date)	Days to Germination	Transplant Date (weeks before (-) or after (+) last frost date)
Vegetables			
Broccoli	10	5 – 10	-3
Cabbage	10	5 – 8	-3
Cauliflower	10	5 – 10	-3
Collards or Kale	10	5 – 8	-3
Leeks	10	5 – 10	-2
Onions	10	5 – 8	-2
Parsley	10	10 – 15	-3
Celery	8	14 – 21	+2
Lettuce	8	2 – 3	-4
Chives	6 – 10	7 – 14	3
Basil	6 – 8	7 – 10	+2
Marjoram	6 – 8	8 – 14	3
Dill	6	21 – 28	+2
Eggplant	6	10 – 14	-2
Peppers	6	10 – 15	+2
Tomatoes	6	7 – 10	+2
Summer Squash	3 – 4	7 – 10	+2
Flowers			
Lobelia	10	14 – 21	+2
Petunias	10	7 – 10	+2
Calendulas	8	7 – 10	-2
Snapdragons	8	7 – 10	-2
Four-O'Clocks	6	7 – 12	+2
Nicotiana	6	14 – 21	+2
Stock	6	7 – 10	+2
Strawflowers	6	3 – 5	+2
Cosmos	4	3 – 5	+2
Marigolds	4	3 – 5	+4
Zinnias	4	3 – 5	+2

Still, don't be afraid to plant more seeds than you think you'll need. (I sure do.) They may not all germinate, and you can always thin out the smallest ones later. If you end up planting more than one type of plant in a tray, choose ones that have about the same germination time and transplant date. And label each section!

It's now time to set your trays in that warm spot you picked and to make absolutely sure you keep them moist. Check them every single day because the minute some pale seed heads start to pop out of the ground, the rules change. You're now dealing with . . .

Seedlings

You've brought these babies into the world; now how can you turn them into strong and sturdy plants eager to enter the garden?

Light

I know I started the seed sequence with soil, but I'm going to change the order here, because the very first thing you need to do for those sprouted seeds is **give them light.** Lots of it. Otherwise, you'll end up with wimpy, leggy, floppy, and — well — downright *embarrassing* seedlings.

Now, some people manage to give their starts enough light by sticking them in a south-facing windowsill. That has never worked well for me. If you try it, be sure to rotate the plants every day or so (they'll always grow toward the window), and try setting up white or tin-foil reflectors around the sides of your containers to bounce more light onto the plants.

For most of us, the better way to go is to set up some long fluorescent lights. Nix to using regular, incandescent lightbulbs — 90 percent of their energy gets lost to heat, and they don't have the right spectrum of light for plant growth, anyway. Use a pair of fluorescent tubes, the longer the better (the light is weakest at the ends). You don't need to buy those special grow-light tubes; regular fluorescent will do fine. (Actually, evidence suggests that for the *best* possible light, you should use one of each.)

You can rig your own light-fixture setup out of chains or wood: just hang the chains from cup hooks so the lights will be adjustable. You want the light practically **right on top of the plants** — no kidding, no more than an inch or two away — so you need to be able to raise the light (or lower your containers) as the seedlings grow.

Give them lots of light — sixteen hours a day is fine. Plants that don't have enough light will grow up leggy, with long stems but few leaves.

Moisture

You kept your seeds constantly moist; but once your seedlings are up and at 'em, you want to moderate that a bit. **Begin watering them slightly less often.** Once they're a few inches tall, let the top half-inch or so of soil actually have a chance to dry out between waterings.

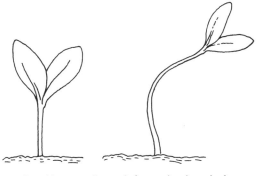

A healthy seedling (left) and a low-light, leggy seedling

Why? Too much moisture encourages root rot or **damping off,** the infamous fungus that can fell your seedlings right at ground level. So water a little less frequently, but more deeply when you do. You can also discourage damping off by making sure the air around your plants is well ventilated instead of stagnant.

Temperature

"Start seeds warm; grow seedlings cool." That's a classic seed starter's saying. Seedlings can grow well at air temperatures between 60° and 70°F. They don't have to have that incubator environment any more once they've "hatched." Besides, if you have to grow plants in a low-light environment where they might tend to be leggy, keeping them a little cool will encourage them to grow more slowly, but also more compactly.

Now that I've given you that obligatory advice, let me admit that, far as I can tell, continued bottom heat makes for quick growth, the same as it did for quick germination. So if you want your starts to grow quickly (and you're supplying them with enough light to support such vertical precociousness), go to it.

Warning: they might grow so fast that they'll be ready to plant out before you had planned to. Also, you'll want to be extra sure to "harden off" such spoiled seedlings before transplanting. (You — of course — don't need me to remind you that we already covered that topic back in Chapter 7.)

Soil/Fertilization

OK, I told you seeds don't need feed — but seedlings do. It's time to start giving them some liquid nutrition, especially if you planted them in plain vermiculite. (Starts planted in such nutritionless media would be prime candidates for pricking out — discussed below.) You can use Rapid Grow or Miracle Gro. Or if you prefer an organic feed, a garden-center kelp or fish emulsion works well (but is a little odoriferous).

Start at half strength, 1½ teaspoons per gallon of water. Feed seedlings no more than twice a week. As they get bigger, you can up the dosage to full strength, 1 tablespoon per gallon.

Let me assure you that proper fertilization is crucial. I know; I've made mistakes at both extremes. In my early ignorance, I didn't fertilize at all — and wondered, with an expression of being-betrayed-by-my-plants in my voice, why my seedlings always ended up puny and pale. Once I learned the obvious errors of my ways, I naturally overfertilized to compensate, dumping a whole gallon of fishy water on two flats of plants.

The leaves developed burned-white spots and began to go limp. Concerned, I did the natural thing — gave them *more* fertilizer. The poor dears were about ready to go to that great greenhouse in the sky — when somebody tipped me off to my mistake. So spare your seedlings from Stone's errors and remember: too much of a good thing is no better than none at all.

What To Do with Seedlings

As I mentioned earlier, many growers prick out their young seedlings — that is, transplant them to new growing trays once they have developed their first **true leaves**. (The first leaves that appear are the **seed leaves**.) "Two-stepping" your starts is not essential, but it does have some advantages. It allows you to start a lot of seeds, then thin to the best ones. You can have one type of

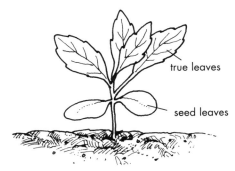

Handle tiny starts by their seed leaves.

container for starting, and another, deeper one with more fertile soil for growing. (You could add some fine compost, say, to growing trays.) And many plants even seem to thrive on the inadvertent root pruning caused by transplanting.

To prick out, make sure the soil is moist but not soggy, and then slice a section of starts out of the tray and rest them on a damp cloth. Keep those roots as covered and moist as possible. Then, with a butter knife or a fork, carefully work one plant free and pick it up by its *seed* leaves (not its true leaves, not its stem, not its root — you don't want to risk damaging those). You may be able to separate tiny rootlets by gently shaking a small cluster of seedlings.

Set each plant in a small hole, as deep up the stem as before or maybe a little deeper. Pack the soil around it gently, and water well to assure good soil-to-root contact. Space these seedlings 2 to 3 inches apart. If they start to wilt right after transplanting, don't deluge with water, but let them rest in a shady spot for a day or so. They should perk back up.

Note: if you don't prick out, but raise your starts in a flat all the way to transplant stage, you'll probably need to thin them at some point to keep them from getting overcrowded

and leggy. The best way to do this is to **snip the reject plants at the soil line with scissors** rather than yank them out, which can disturb the roots of the plants you want to keep.

Fending Off Damping Off

What if the dreaded (cue ominous music) damping off disease strikes your starts, felling your seedlings overnight like a mini-clearcutter gone wild? Quick, throw out the infected seedlings! Every one! Then make sure those that didn't get infected have plenty of ventilation and not too much water. Don't reuse any infected soil mix (in fact, err on the side of caution: don't *ever* reuse any soil mix). And wash your containers with a bleach solution and let them air dry before using them again.

Actually, if you use a sterile soil mix, you probably won't have any problem with damping off. But if it ever strikes once, take steps to reduce the chances of getting it again. Give your next starts occasional mistings with solutions of kelp or chamomile tea, both of which seem to act as good fungal preventatives. And consider laying a ¼-inch layer of sand or vermiculite on top of your seed containers to promote drainage at the base of the plants' stems.

Home, Sweet Garden Home

Eventually, your seedlings will be a couple of inches tall, the weather will be warm, and you'll be ready to transplant your starts to their true and final home: your garden. (You will then — why, of course — follow all the procedures covered in "Transplanting," Chapter 7.)

This last act of seed starting, the tender transfer of your carefully nurtured seedlings out into the real world, is always a warm and touching one. It's also a moment of real accomplishment and pride. Why, you should cherish it like a badge of honor. Those little starts show that you are now a gardening veteran. No more beginner mistakes for you. You're an official graduate of the school of basic gardening mistakes, ready to move on and make more advanced mistakes!

But don't rush. Pull your trowel out of the dirt for a minute, sit back, and just plain enjoy the moment. You've earned it.

Besides, you'll soon be so busy with all the weeding, watering, and debugging to come that you may not get to relax again until fall.

But hey, friend, that's gardening!

AFTERWORD

I'd like to thank you for sticking with me all the way through this book. Strange as this may sound, I feel that I've gotten to know you a little — and I've enjoyed the acquaintance. If you make only half the mistakes I've made, why, you'll turn out to be twice the gardener I am!

Now that we're about to part company, I want to wish you the best in all your gardening endeavors. You will, of course, have plenty of failures, even when *you* don't goof up. The weather will pull pranks your plants positively won't appreciate. Bugs or varmints will, on occasion, get a little overzealous with their defoliation programs. And you'll run across some plants that won't deign to grow for you no matter how hard you try.

But a real gardener takes the manure in life and turns it into compost, right? So don't let the failures get to you. Focus on the fun part. Enjoy the joys. After all, the most important thing we ever grow in our gardens . . . is ourselves.

God bless you,

Pat Stone

INDEX

Page references in *italics* indicate illustrations; bold indicates charts.

A

Acidity, of soil, adjusting, 34
Advice, importance of obtaining
    local, 13
Alfalfa, 59, 67, 96
Alkalinity, of soil, adjusting, 34
Alstromeria, 83
Animal control, 99–110
Aphids, 88
Assassin bugs, 95
Australian lady beetles, 95

B

Baking soda spray, 116
Barricades, for controlling pests,
    93, *93*
Beanpole teepee, *121*
Bean seedlings, 45
Beets, 56
Beginning mistakes
    letting gardening become a
        chore, 16–17
    not keeping records, 15–16
    not obtaining local advice, 13
    not protecting against pests, 16
    planting only once, 15
    planting too early, 14, 16
    starting too big, 11–12
Beneficial insects, 94–96
Bindweed, 82
Birds, 96, 107
Blackberries, pruning, 150, *150*
Blood meal, 36
Blueberries, pruning, 150
Bonemeal, 37, 126
Bordeaux mix, 116
Boron, 38
Braconid wasps, 95
Brambles, pruning, 150, *150*

Broadcasting seed, 41–42
B.T. *(Bacillus thuringiensas),* 97
Buckwheat, 58, 59, 96
Buds, types of, 143
Bulbs, 125–28, *126*
Burdock, 82

C

Cabbage fly, 93
Cabbageworms, 97
Calcium, 38
Canada thistle, 82
Carrots, 27, 42, 43, 56, 119, 121
Cart, wheelbarrow versus, 23
Cartenoids, 49
Castor beans, 104
Caterpillars, 97
Cations, 62
Cats, 103–4, 109
Chenopodiaceae, 56
Chicken manure, 36
Chickweed, 83, *84*
Chlorine, 38
Clover, 57, 59, 96
Colorado potato beetles, 88, 92
Companion planting, 90–91
Compositae, 96
Compost
    activator, 64
    air, 64–65
    brown matter, 64
    cool, 63, 64
    disease control and use of, 113
    green matter, 64
    hot, 63–64, 67, 156
    prejudices against, 61–63
    soil added to, 64
    tea, 116, 123
    trench, 68

    what not to use for, 68
Composters, commercial, 68
Compost pile, building a, 65–66,
    65, 66
Compost problems
    doesn't heat up, 67
    lack of materials, 67–68
    smells, 67
Copper, 38
Corn, weeds among, 7
Cottonseed meal, 36
Cover cropping, 56–60, 96, 135
Crabgrass, 83
Crop rotation, 56, 91, 115
Cruciferae, 56
Cucumber beetles, 90, 98
Cucumbers, 56
Cucurbitaceae, 56
Cutworms, 93

D

Damping off, 159, 160
Dandelions, 82
Deadheading, 122, 127, 147
Deciduous trees, pruning, 146
Deer, 102–3, *103*, 110
Diatomaceous earth (DE), 97
Digging. *See* Ground preparation
Diseases, controlling and preventing
    compost and, 113
    covering plants, 115–16
    crop rotation and, 115
    growing resistant varieties, 115
    keeping foliage dry, 113–14
    mulch and, 114
    preventive measures, 112–16
    problem with ignoring, 112
    sanitation and, 113
    sprays for, 116

Sprays, to control diseases, 116
Sprinklers, use of, 72
Squash vine borer, 94
Staking plants, 119–20, *120, 121*
Starting seeds indoors, 152–58
Stellaria media, 83
Stirrup hoe, 21, 23, *23,* 80–81, *80*
Straw versus hay, 38, 68
Succession plantings, 15, 123–24
Sulphur, 38
Sulpo-mag, 38
Sunlight
    proper amount needed, 4–5, *4*
    sloping sites and, 9, *9*
Supporting plants, 119–20, *120, 121*

T

Tanglefoot, 94
Thinning, 119, 121
Tillers, types of, 26–27, *26*
Tilling, 25–30
    fall, 135
    problem when soil is too wet,
        24–25
    reasons for removing sod
        completely before, 25
    testing soil moisture, 25, *25*
Tilthing, 27, *27*
Timing chart
    for starting seeds indoors, 156,
        157
    for sowing seed outdoors, **44**
Tomatoes, 56
Tools
    care of, 22, 113, 136–37
    cost versus quality of, 18–19
    garden fork, 20
    garden rake, 21
    hand versus power, 19–20
    hoes, 21, 23, *23,* 80–81, *80*
    hoses, 19, 23
    sharpening, 22, *22*
    shovel versus spade, 21, 25
    sowing, 39
    trowel, 21
    wheelbarrow versus cart, 23

Transplants/transplanting
    buying tips, 51
    buying too many, 47
    digging hole for, 50, *50*
    legginess or yellowing, 51
    seedlings, 159–61, *160*
    setting plants in the hole, 50–51
    setting plants out too early, 48
    setting plants out without
        hardening off, 48–49
    sheltering, 51–52
    timing of, 49–50
    watering, 50, 51
Traps, 93–94, 105, *105*
Trees and shrubs
    fruit trees, pruning, 148–49, *148*
    mulching, 132–33
    planting tips, 129–33, *131*
    protection from pests, *107*
    pruning shrubs, 144–45, *145*
    pruning trees, 145–49, *146, 147,*
        148
    sawing off limbs, 147, 147
    selecting, 128
    site location for, 128–29
    staking, *131,* 132
    watering, 131, 133
    when to plant, 129
Trellis, 120, *120*
Trench composting, 68
Trenching, 39–40, *40*
Trichogramma wasps, 95
Trowel, 21
True leaves, 159, *160*

U

Umbelliferae, 56, 96
Undercropping, 60

V

Vetch, 57, 59, 96

W

Wasps, beneficial, 95
Watering
    to control pests, 97

determining amount needed,
    70–72, *70*
drip irrigation, 73–74, *73, 74*
emitter systems, 23, 74
fall, 137
in-ground milk jug for, 75, *75*
mulch used to conserve water, 73
newly planted trees and shrubs,
    131, 133
seedlings, 158–59
seeds, 42–44, 71
seeds started indoors, 154–55
soaker hoses for, 23, 74, *74*
soil moisture testing, 25, *25,*
    70, *71*
sprinklers for, 72
time of day for, 71, 72–73
tips for conserving water, 75
transplants, 50, 51
wand, *74, 75*
Water problems
    drainage problems, 6–9, *8*
    surface runoff problems, 8
Water sprouts, 148
Weeds/weeding, 24, 36, 111
    cover crops to eliminate, 58
    cultivation versus, 79
    eating, 85
    importance of, 80
    killers, 82
    perennial, 82–83, *82*
    reworking soil to control, 29–30
    stirrup hoe for controlling, 21,
        23, *23,* 80–81, *80*
    tips on, 83–85
    views toward, 78–79
    when to do, 81
Wheelbarrow versus cart, 23
Windbreaks, 8–9, *8,* 75, 138, *138*
Winter, preparation for, 135–38
Wire cages, 120
Wood ashes, 38
Woodchucks, 105, *105,* 109–10

Z

Zinc, 38

Other Storey Titles You Will Enjoy

The Able Gardener: Overcoming Barriers of Age & Physical Limitations, by Kathleen Yeomans, R.N. How to begin, or continue, a lifetime of successful gardening in spite of physical challenges. 296 pages. Paperback. $16.95 US/NCR. Order #789-0. Hardcover. $27.95 US/NCR. Order #790-4.

The Big Book of Gardening Skills, by Editors of Garden Way Publishing. A comprehensive guide to growing flowers, fruits, herbs, vegetables, shrubs, and lawns. 352 pages. Paperback. $18.95 US/$26.50 CAN. Order # 795-5. Hardcover. $29.95 US/$41.95 CAN. Order #796-3.

Bugs, Slugs, & Other Thugs: Controlling Garden Pests Organically, by Rhonda Massingham Hart. Hundreds of ways to stop pests without risk to the user or the environment. 224 pages. Paperback $9.95 US/$13.95 CAN. Order #664-9.

Bulbs: Four Seasons of Beautiful Blooms, by Lewis and Nancy Hill. A season-by-season approach to adding the beauty and color of bulbs to home and garden. 224 pages. Paperback. $18.95 US/$26.50 CAN. Order #877-3. Hardcover. $28.95 US/$40.95 CAN. Order #878-1.

Carrots Love Tomatoes: Secrets of Companion Planting for Successful Gardening, by Louise Riotte. How to grow and where to plant vegetables, in a book sprinkled with anecdotes, quotations, and recipes. 224 pages. Paperback. $9.95 US/$13.95 CAN. Order #064-0.

Caring for Perennials, by Janet Macunovich. Use a practical, hands-on approach and time-saving techniques and grow a spectacular perennial garden. 192 pages. Paperback. $17.95 US/$24.95 CAN. Order #957-5.

Cold-Climate Gardening: How to Extend Your Growing Season by at Least 30 Days, by Lewis Hill. Chapters on vegetables, fruits, nuts, and herbs. 320 pages. Paperback. $14.95 US/$20.95 CAN. Order #441-7.

Dirt-Cheap Gardening: Hundreds of Ways to Save Money in Your Garden, by Rhonda Massingham Hart. A compilation of years of experience and tested ideas for saving money and cutting costs. 144 pages. Paperback. $9.95 US/$13.95 CAN. Order #898-6.

Easy Garden Design: 12 Simple Steps to Creating Successful Gardens and Landscapes, by Janet Macunovich. Includes site assesment and combinations of plantings to create a workable and attractive garden and landscape. 176 pages. Paperback. $14.95 US/$20.95 CAN. Order #791-2.

Fences for Pasture and Garden, by Gail Damerow. The complete guide to choosing, planning, and building today's best fences. 160 pages. Paperback. $14.95 US/$20.95 CAN. Order #753-X. Hardcover. $24.95 US/$34.95 CAN. Order #754-8.

The Gardener's Complete Q & A, by Editors of Garden Way Publishing. Answers to thousands of often-asked questions on lawns, landscaping, perennials, annuals, herbs, fruits, and vegetables. 736 pages. Hardcover. $39.95 US/$55.95 CAN. Order #904-4.

READING LIST

167

A Garden of Wildflowers: 101 Native Species and How to Grow Them, by Henry Art. An authoritative and comprehensive book, including full descriptions of each plant. 304 pages. Paperback. $18.95 US/$26.50 CAN. Order #405-0.

Green Thumb Wisdom: Garden Myths Revealed!, by Doc and Katy Abraham. Doc and Katy explode common fallacies while providing accurate answers to growers' most frequent questions and problems. 144 pages. Paperback. $12.95 US/$17.95 CAN. Order #928-1

The "Have-More" Plan: A Little Land--A Lot of Living, by Ed and Carolyn Robinson. Learn how to find good land, build a working homestead, grow vegetables and fruits, raise livestock, build farm structures, and more. 72 pages. Paperback. $9.95 US/$13.95 CAN. Order #024-1.

The Herb Gardener: A Guide for All Seasons, by Susan McClure. Complete instructions on every conceivable aspect of herbs so the reader can successfully grow and use 75 different herbs all year long. 236 pages. Paperback. $19.95 US/$27.95 CAN. Order #873-0. Hardcover. $29.95 US/$39.95 CAN. Order #910-9.

Joy of Gardening, by Dick Raymond. A bestselling gardening "bible" that shares proven techniques for a bigger harvest with less work. 384 pages. Paperback. $19.95 US/$27.95 CAN. Order #319-4.

Just the Facts! Dozens of Garden Charts--Thousands of Gardening Answers, by Editors of Garden Way. Covers vegetables, herbs, shrubs, bulbs, annuals, ground covers, wildflowers, and more. 224 pages. Paperback. $16.95 US/$23.75 CAN. Order #867-6.

Let it Rot! The Gardener's Guide to Composting (Revised and Updated), by Stu Campbell. Simplifies the technical terminology to make composting easy, and provides information on selecting and combining the right materials. 144 pages. Paperback. $8.95 US/$12.75 CAN. Order #635-5.

The Mulch Book: A Complete Guide for Gardeners (Revised and Updated), by Stu Campbell. Details how to make and use bark, stones, hay, compost, and other materials as a barrier for keeping weeds out and beneficial elements in. 160 pages. Paperback. $9.95 US/ $13.95 CAN. Order #659-2.

Pruning Simplified (Updated), by Lewis Hill. This timeless guide to pruning is based on the premise that pruning, if done right, strengthens and rejuvenates plants. 208 pages. Paperback. $14.95 US/$20.95 CAN. Order #417-4.

Tips for the Lazy Gardener, by Linda Tilgner. Hundreds of valuable suggestions for every gardener who wants to cut down on weeding and enjoy gardening more. 128 pages. Paperback. $6.95 US/$9.95 CAN. Order #390-9.

Warm-Climate Gardening: Tips, Techniques,Plans, Projects for Humid or Dry Conditions, by Barbara Pleasant. The author explains how to choose drought-resistant plants, schedule maintenance chores, and exploit cool intervals within the warm-climate gardening year. 208 pages. Paperback. $12.95 US/$17.95 CAN. Order #818-8.

■ ■ ■ ■ ■ ■ ■ ■ ■

These books and other Storey books are available at your bookstore, farm store, garden center, or directly from Storey Publishing, Schoolhouse Road, Pownal, Vermont 05261, or by calling **1-800-441-5700.**